A Social
History of Tea

A Social History of Tea

Jane Pettigrew

THE NATIONAL TRUST

First published in Great Britain in 2001 by
National Trust Enterprises Ltd.,
36 Queen Anne's Gate, London SW1H 9AS

http://www.nationaltrust.org.uk/bookshop

British Library Cataloguing in Publication Data
A catalogue record for this book is available from
the British Library

ISBN 0 7078 0289 X

Picture research by Philippa Reynolds
Designed by Sarah Mattinson at TRUE
Production management by Bob Towell
Printed and bound in China
Phoenix Offset

*Half title: Late eighteenth-century satinwood
tea chest from Fenton House in Hampstead.*

*Frontispiece: Thomas Smith and his Family,
painted in 1733 by Robert West. A servant
stands ready to pour more water from the silver
kettle into the tiny teapot. Milk and sugar are
served in a silver jug and bowl.*

Contents

Madge Crichton, an Edwardian maidservant serving tea, a job that would have demanded her skills and a steady hand on most afternoons of the week.

INTRODUCTION

For almost twenty years I have been fascinated by the story of tea. Although there have been many studies of different aspects, I have aimed in this book to cover the subject in greater depth and breadth, and thus concentrated on the story of tea drinking in Britain. It is extraordinary how tea has permeated through so many different areas of our national history since the seventeenth century. Pick almost any period or any topic, and tea is almost certain to make its appearance – the repeating theme of the beverage as a cure for all ills, the rules and rituals of eighteenth-century tea drinking, the introduction in the 1840s of the very British 'afternoon tea' that led to the opening of tea rooms as places where, for the first time, respectable women could eat out unaccompanied, the development of the tea gown and the eccentricity of the tango tea dance, to cite just a few. And mention tea today, of course, and absolutely everyone has something to say on the matter.

During the first one hundred years or so, the expensive beverage was almost exclusively an indulgence enjoyed by the upper classes, and thus associated with stately homes, fine oriental porcelains, elegant European silverwares and gracious manners. As the price was reduced, it gradually became the drink of the masses until people from all walks of life and all social classes drank it at almost any time of the day. While other European countries, after a brief flirtation with the Chinese herb, turned to coffee as their staple drink, Britain's commitment to tea grew steadily.

My research over the years has taken me to all corners of the United Kingdom. I have pried into the private diaries of aristocrats and farmers, merchants and ordinary working folk. I have delved into the household accounts from grand mansions and ordinary suburban and rural homes. I have pored over books and family papers, newspapers and journals in libraries and record offices, private collections, and the archives of tea companies.

The National Trust is, of course, a natural source of information for this subject since it was in the closets and withdrawing rooms of many of the historic houses that now belong to the Trust that tea was drunk. It is impossible individually to thank all the people employed by the Trust who have been kind enough to help me in my search. But my special thanks go to the National Trust's Publisher, Margaret Willes, whose incredible historical knowledge and clarity of vision helped to shape this book. I am deeply indebted to her for all her help in both researching and writing the text. My thanks also go to her editorial assistant, Philippa Reynolds, whose patience and calm support while working on the enormous task of picture research and all the day-to-day chores involved has been astonishing. I would also like to thank Oliver Garnett, the Guidebook Editor, for his help with detailed historical information, and Ed Gibbons in the National Trust Photographic Library.

Thanks also go to the staff in art galleries, museums, libraries, record offices and local history centres all over Britain who helped me find relevant books and papers. For their help with illustrations, I would like particularly to thank Peter Brown at Fairfax House in York, Frank Dickens, Leonard Griffin, Diana James, Sam Twining, Nigel Temple and John Weatherstone. And finally thank you to all my friends, who always understood when my work took precedence over social events, and who were a source of constant support during the nine concentrated months in which this book was written.

Jane Pettigrew, December 2000

Samuel Pepys, who recorded his first cup of tea in his diary. He also noted sitting for this portrait by John Hales on 30 March 1666. Pepys took great delight in the exotic commodities being imported into London, and for his portrait chose to wear his Indian gown, an informal garment of golden brown silk cut like a kimono.

The Seventeenth Century

THE FIRST TEA IN ENGLAND

On 25 September 1660, Samuel Pepys recorded in his diary that, in the middle of his working day as the Navy's Clerk of the Acts, 'he did send for a Cupp of Tee (a China drink), of which I had never drank before'. This first cup came five months after the restoration of the English monarchy and just a few weeks after he had travelled by ship to accompany Charles II back to England from exile in The Hague.

Tea was just one of a multitude of exotic commodities arriving in the port of London in the middle of the seventeenth century on ships of the East India Company. For 60 years, since Queen Elizabeth I had granted them their charter, they had been exploring the Far East in their quest for a route to the spice islands. In the company's almost relentless attempts to secure regular supplies of nutmeg – thought at the time to ward off the evils of the plague – they had waged ferocious battles with the Spanish, Dutch and Portuguese for territory, dominance of the seas, and trading rights. And in their travels, they had acquired samples of all manner of unusual goods and carried them home in their battered ships. Back in England, silks and calico, tobacco, sugar, chocolate, coffee, dried tropical fruits, oranges, porcelains and jewels tempted the coins from the pockets of the wealthy and caught the covetous eye and imagination of those whose pounds and pennies were needed for more basic and essential goods.

Those who could afford them – government officials like Pepys, aristocrats, members of the royal family – were fascinated and excited by the taste of the new foods and drinks, seduced by the brilliant colours and textures of the fabrics, enticed by the fine translucency of the porcelains. But, since those who traded and purchased these foreign luxuries did not fully comprehend their nature or origin, names were often muddled and misleading. Indian cottons were referred to as chintz because they were thought to come from China, wallpapers from China were thought to be Indian. It mattered little: the fact that they came from distant lands was enough.

Improved communications enabled these goods to find their way, with travelling merchants, pedlars, and provincial shopkeepers, to areas outside London. What had previously been a regional economy in which local goods were sold locally had begun to develop into a nationally integrated marketplace. Large towns became commercial centres with shops of all kinds, legal services, medical practitioners, estate agents, theatres and public assembly rooms. Gentlemen and wealthy farmers would travel regularly to town, sometimes bringing their families to combine business and leisure.

Although the brief note in Pepys' diary was the first mention of tea actually being consumed in England, he was certainly not the first person to hear about the new herb from the East. The earliest advertisement in England for the sale of tea appeared in 1658 in the 23–30 September edition of *Mercurius Politicus*, a London weekly newspaper. This announced 'That Excellent, and by all Physitians approved, China Drink, called by the Chineans, Tcha, by other Nations

Tay alias Tee, is sold at the Sultaness-head, a Cophee-house in Sweetings Rents by the Royal Exchange, London.' By the following year, tea was generally available around London, as Thomas Rugg mentioned in his *Diurnal*, 1659–61: 'November 14th 1659 And theire ware also att this time a Turkish drink to bee sould, almost evry street, called coffee, and a nother kind of drink called tee, and also a drink called Chacolate, which was a very harty drink.'

The business records of Thomas Garway, the first London merchant to deal in tea, also suggest that it was on sale in London prior to 1657, the year that he first traded it. His papers explain that it was very expensive and that 'in respect of its former scarceness and dearness, it hath been only used as Regalia in high Treatments and Entertainments, and Presents made thereof to Princes and Grandees'.

A century later, in 1756, Jonas Hanway attributed the arrival of tea to two members of the aristocracy: 'Lord Arlington and Lord Offory were the persons who brought it from Holland in 1666; their ladies then became passionately enamoured with it as a new thing: their example recommended it to the fine women of those days ... .' Hanway was not quite correct historically, but he was right in acknowledging the use of tea at this time only amongst the upper classes. It was far too expensive for anyone but the wealthy.

The earliest advertisement for tea in Mercurius Politicus, 23–30 September 1658. *From the very outset, the drink was commended on grounds of health.*

That Excellent, and by all Physitians approved, *China Drink*, called by the *Chineans, Tcha*, by other Nations *Tay alias Tee*, is sold at the *Sultaness-head*, a Cophee-house in *Sweetings Rents* by the Royal Exchange, *London*.

THE ORIGINS OF TEA

Indian mythology claims that tea originated in the north of India and that tea bushes were transplanted to China's Sichuan province in the sixth century BC. But Chinese legend sets the story of tea's discovery long before that, in the days of the Emperor Shen Nung, who is said to have lived round about 2737BC. As well as being credited with inventing a system of agriculture, this mythical figure is believed to have been a herbalist who experimented with many plants to discover their character and medicinal benefits. However, the *Medical Book* attributed to him was not actually written until the first and second centuries AD, and a reference to tea was only added in the seventh century AD. That addition claimed that tea 'is good for tumours or abscesses that come about the head, or for ailments of the bladder. It dissipates heat caused by Phlegms, or inflammations of the chest. It quenches the thirst. It lessens the desire for sleep. It gladdens and cheers the heart.'

Sichuan, in the west of China, may have been the first province to grow and drink tea, but with increasing interest and demand, cultivation of the plant gradually spread to other areas until almost the entire southern half of China was producing tea.

Over the centuries, the Chinese used various methods of processing and brewing the leaves they gathered. In the very earliest days of tea drinking, they boiled the fresh, unprocessed leaves in water to give a bitter, unappetising brew. Next, the dried and crushed leaves were boiled in water. By the ninth century, the freshly picked leaves were steamed and compressed into flat cakes, which were

strung together and baked until hard and dry. To brew a bowl of tea, the cakes were pounded into small pieces and boiled. By this time, China was trading widely with countries to the west, east and north, and brick tea, made in the same way for export, was used as currency in exchange for imported goods.

During the tenth, eleventh and twelfth centuries, whipped green tea became fashionable and it was this method of whisking the finely powdered, dried green leaves into hot water that eventually developed into the central feature of the Japanese tea ceremony.

Knowledge of the plant and the infusion had travelled to Japan in the eighth century when a Buddhist monk, Dengyo Daishi, who had been studying in China, carried seeds back home and planted them in the garden of his monastery. When the Japanese emperor tasted green tea made from the leaves of the new plants a few years later, he gave instructions for plantations to be established in five provinces around Kyoto, then the capital of Japan.

In China, from about AD1300, the fashion for powdered tea gave way to the brewing method used today – that of infusing loose processed leaves in hot or boiling water. It was this method that early European travellers encountered, so it was the brewing method that was adopted when Chinese merchants started trading with Europe.

Details from eighteenth-century Chinese wallpaper now decorating the Chinese Chippendale Bedroom at Saltram in Devon. These show the first stages in the 'Story of Tea': labourers with wooden buckets and pails watering the tea plants; withering the leaves; tasters sampling the tea, with a teapot and cups in the background; treading down the leaves in large baskets, ready for packing (see also pages 14-15).

The first trade links with Europe were established in 1557 when the Portuguese reached China by sea. By 1619, the English East India Company had sailed as far as Japan and was on good terms with the Chinese court, but became distracted from its business efforts by a bloody power struggle with the Dutch for monopoly of the spice trade. Four years later, the Dutch had won and the English were forced to withdraw to mainland India and its surrounding islands. With no base in China, the company met with little success in its early attempts to trade and no tea was imported to England by the East India Company until 1669.

However, Mr R. Wickham, an agent for the company on the Japanese island of Hirado, wrote to a colleague at the Chinese port of Macao in 1615 asking him to send a pot of 'the best sort of chaw'. The English collector of travellers' tales, Samuel Purchas, had enough information from various sources to write of the Chinese in *Purchas His Pilgrimes*, published in 1625: 'They use much the powder of a certaine herbe called chia of which they put as much as a walnut shell may containe, into a dish of Porcelane, and drink it with hot water' and he explains that it was used 'in all entertainments in Iapon and China'. The Cornish traveller, Peter Mundy, wrote in 1637 during a

visit to Fukien in the Chinese province of Fujian, 'the people there gave us a certain Drinke called Chaa which is only water with a kind of herb boyled in it'.

Even brewers knew about it. *A Treatise on Warm Beer*, written in England in 1641 to encourage the consumption of warm, rather than cold beverages, quotes an Italian priest as having discovered that 'They of China do for the most part drink the strained liquor of a herb called Chia hot'. And in 1659, Daniel Sheldon, another employee of the East India Company based at Balsore, had written to a colleague at Bandel asking for a sample of tea. Sheldon wished to send it to his uncle, Dr Gilbert Sheldon, the Archbishop of Canterbury. 'I must desire you to procure the chaw, if possible. I care not what it cost, 'tis for a good uncle of mine, Dr Sheldon, whom some body hath perswaded to studdy the divinity of that herbe, leafe, or what else it is; and I am soe obliged to satisfy his curiosity that I could willingly undertake a viage to Japan or China to doe it.'

We know that both the Portuguese and Dutch were importing tea into Europe from their trading bases in Macao on the Canton river and Bantam on the island of Java as early as 1610. By 1611, the Dutch were also trading tea from Japan. The Directors of the Dutch East India Company wrote a letter to their

Governor-General in Java saying 'As tea begins to come into use with some of our people, we expect some jars of Chinese, as well as Japanese tea with each ship.' But the English were having no success in their efforts to export tea from China, and seem also to have ignored the possibilities of shipping it from Japan, despite the temporary establishment of

a trading post on Hirado and the fact that other Europeans were already trading tea from there.

Whatever the reasons for the lack of trade in tea by the English, it was the Dutch who were responsible for importing the first very small consignments to reach London in 1657. These were carried on English-registered ships in compliance with the Navigation Act of 1651, but were traded by the Dutch. So, when the East India Company wished to present a casket of tea to Charles II and his queen, Catharine of Braganza, in 1664, they had to buy it from the Dutch merchants.

A Dutch East Indiaman at anchor amongst smaller transport vessels on the Maas at Dordrecht, from a painting of the 1650s by Aelbert Cuyp (1620–91).

THE JOURNEY TO ENGLAND

The passage from China to London of those early consignments of tea was complicated and protracted. Farmers all over China grew tea as one of various crops on their smallholdings. The first two pickings of the season, gathered in mid-April and June, yielded the best quality and were mainly exported. Third and fourth pluckings from the later summer months were generally kept for home consumption. The smallholders sold their tea to local dealers who sampled them and put together a 'chop' of roughly 620–30 chests. The 'chops' were then transported across mountains by coolies to wholesale centres where dealers from China and Europe gathered to select the teas they wanted. From here the tea was shipped in canal boats on a highly developed system of inland waterways down to the main port at Canton, 40 miles inland on the River Zhujiang. The journey from the remote mountain areas where the tea was produced could take at least six weeks and could cover anything up to 1,200 miles. Hot sun or downpours of rain could easily destroy the tea and sometimes the entire year's crop was lost due to such adverse conditions. By September, the spring teas had usually arrived in the ports where a second selection process took place, with agents acting for the various European companies. The East Indiamen set sail with their cargoes of tea, silk, spices, and porcelain in January, reaching London in the winter or following spring. So the teas that were eventually sold in seventeenth-century London were never less than 18 to 24 months old.

Details from eighteenth-century Chinese wallpaper now decorating the Chinese Chippendale Bedroom at Saltram. These show later stages in the 'Story of Tea': opposite page, sawing and planing wood to make tea crates; below, binding up the baskets; transporting baskets down river to trading bases (see also pages 10-11).

From the days of the earliest shipments, both black and green tea were imported. At first all types were referred to by one of three names: 'Tea' or 'tee', derived from the Amoy dialect word *te* and adopted by the Dutch traders who had regular contact with Chinese merchants from Amoy; 'Chaa' was the Cantonese dialect word, used by Portuguese merchants trading out of Macao; 'Bohea' was quickly adopted for black tea, named after the Bohea mountains where it was (and still is) produced. By the 1700s, customers were being offered 20 or so different types, each of which now had its own name.

To help the public understand what they were buying, merchants often published explanations of the goods available. In 1699, John Ovington, Chaplain to King William III, wrote his *Essay upon the Nature and Qualities of Tea*, in which he demonstrated the different sorts and the way in which they were transported:

The first Sort is Bohea, or as the Chinese have it, Voui, which is the little Leaf inclining to black and generally tinges the Water brown, or of a reddish colour. Those in China that are sick, or are very careful of preserving their Health, if they are weak, confine themselves only to this kind of Tea…. The second Sort is Singlo,

or Soumlo with the Chinese; of which there are several kinds, according to the place of Growth, the manner of preparing it, and the Nature of the Tea. One of them is a narrow and long Leaf. The other smaller, and of a blewish green colour, which tastes very crisp when it is chaw'd…. And will endure the Change of Water three or four times. This Tea is brought over in round Totaneg [a kind of metal brought from China] canisters pasted over with paper and inclos'd in a wooden Tub…. The third Sort is Bing, or Imperial Tea. This is a large loose Leaf… 'tis highly esteem'd likewise in China, being sold there at three times the price of the other two. This likewise, as the others, is imported in large thick Totaneg Canisters included in wooden Tubs, or in Baskets made of small Bamboo canes.

An advertisement in the *Tatler* on 10 October 1710 announced: 'Mr Favy's 16s Bohea tea, not much inferior in goodness to the best foreign Bohea tea, is sold by himself only at the "Bell" in Gracechurch Street. Note – the best foreign Bohea is worth 30s a pound: so that what is sold at 20s or 21s must either be faulty tea, or mixed with a proportionate quantity of damaged green or Bohea, the worst of which will remain black after infusion.' A nineteenth-century book explained that bohea was an English corruption of

the words 'woo-e', 'voo-yee' or 'ba-yee', 'some hills of that name about 12 miles in circumference in Fokien, on the borders of Canton province, yielding a common tea of that name …'.

After a very slow start, the East India Company eventually woke up to tea's commercial potential. In 1669, it ordered and shipped the first cargo of 143lb, and in 1670, a further 79lb arrived – both lots arriving from the Company's trading post at Bantam on the island of Java. After that, regular amounts were imported from trading posts at Bantam, Surat, Ganjam and Madras. In 1689, the first lots began to arrive from Amoy in China, with two cargoes carrying, among other goods: 'Tea 150 peculs, halfe in Canisters and ½ in Potts made up in Chests Ye Potts to contain 1 to 4 Cattees of Tea each Pott, extraordinary good, being for England'. 'Pecul' derives from the Malay word 'pikul' meaning 'to carry a heavy load'. 'Cattee' is also Malay and denotes an amount of roughly 1⅔ lb.

Despite the arrival of fairly regular shipments, they were not huge amounts, and the slow progress of the trade suggests that interest among the general population was negligible and that demand remained very small. In 1678, 5,000lb was enough to cause a glut on the London market. Although imports continued, by the end of the 1680s a regular trade with China had still not really been established.

High prices were certainly one reason for this slow development. Thomas Garway's teas sold for prices between 16 shillings and 60 shillings (£3) per pound. In 1666, a housewife 'sent to Bristol for good Brandy and Comfits for it. Paid 31s for the Brandy.... Put by the new China tea, 40s a pound'. The household accounts of 1690 for Mary, Countess of Argyll show that 6 ounces of tea cost £10 16s 0d – more than £26 per pound.

When salaries and wages for the period are taken into consideration, the high cost of tea becomes even more astounding. For example, at Woburn Abbey in Bedfordshire, the country estate of the 5th Earl of Bedford, the bill in 1658 for the entire staff of officials and servants (including casual and full-time maids, cooks, footmen, porters, clerks, watchmen, stable boys, grooms, gardeners, stewards, lawyer and Receiver General) amounted to only £600. The estate lawyer earned £20, and a footman

between £2 and £6 a year. Compare that with £26 for a pound of tea and it becomes clear that it was probably only the Earl and Countess themselves who could afford this new commodity.

William Daniell's eighteenth-century painting of A View of the European factories at Canton. *Agents of the various European companies were responsible for organising cargoes of tea, silks, porcelains, spices, precious stones and lacquers for shipment.*

TEA IN COFFEE HOUSES

The advertisement in *Mercurius Politicus* (page 9) is clear evidence that tea was first sold in the coffee houses of London. Coffee had started arriving in England before tea, with the first coffee house opened in Oxford in 1650 by a man called Jacob. The earliest in London is thought to have opened in 1652 in St Michael's Alley off Cornhill in the City. At first there was a hostile reaction from some local residents because of the smell of the new brew and the number of 'undesirable' people the coffee houses attracted to the neighbourhood. The brewers and vintners saw them as a threat to the beer and wine trade, but most people thoroughly approved of the new trend and the coffee houses quickly became popular meeting places for businessmen. They were rather like gentlemen's clubs, aimed at an all-male upper- and middle-class clientele, each establishment attracting its own particular group of customers – merchants, physicians, politicians, journalists, intellectuals, lawyers, and even clergymen. The Swiss writer, Muralt, in his 1696 publication, *Letters describing the Character and Customs of the English and French Nations*, said, 'In my opinion they are very proper places to find people that a man has business with, or to pass away the time a little more agreeably, perhaps, than he can do at home ... .'

In *The Story of the Country Mouse and the City Mouse*, a satirical poem of 1687, Matthew Prior and Charles Montagu, later Lord Halifax, wrote:

'As I remember', said the sober Mouse,
'I've heard much talk of the Wit's
coffee-house.'
'Thither', says Brindle, 'thou shalt
go and see
Priests sipping coffee, Sparks and
Poets tea;'

The *Intelligence* for 3 January 1664/5 told readers of 'one Constantine, a Grecian, living in Thredneedle-street, over against St Christopher's Church, London, being licensed to sell and retail Coffee, Chocolate, Cherbert, [sherbet was a cold drink made of fruit juice, water and sugar], and Tea'. Another commentator wrote that one coffee-house owner sold 'chocolate and sherberts made in Turkie, of lemon, roses, and violets perfumes; and Tea or Chaa, according to its goodness'. Some also sold a range of alcoholic drinks. One writer – thought to be the Florentine ambassador to London – commented that they sold 'other beverages such as chocolate, sherbert, tea, ale, cock-ale, beer, etc, according to the season'. And another account lists 'tea and aromatick for the sweet-toothed gentleman, betony and rosade-chocolate for the consumptive gallant, Herefordshire readstreak [a kind of cider] made of rotten apples at the Three Cranes, true Brunswick mum [a beer originally brewed from wheat in Brunswick, Germany] brewed at St Catharine's, and ale in penny mugs, not so big as a taylor's thimble'.

Mrs Centlivre set the first scenes of her play of 1718, *A Bold Strike for a Wife*, in Jonathan's Coffee House in Exchange Alley. As the characters discuss business and news, the coffee boys move around the room calling, 'Fresh coffee, gentlemen! Fresh coffee! Bohea tea, gentlemen!' The use of the word 'fresh' is questionable since during the early years of tea and coffee drinking, the tax due was imposed by excise men who visited each morning to assess how much was to be served during the day. Barrels of tea, coffee and chocolate were prepared in advance and kept hot by the fire until customers placed their orders. In 1750, Thomas Short commented in *Discourses on Tea, Sugar, Milk, Made-Wines, Spirits, Punch, Tobacco* that this caused 'no small prejudice to the Liquor and inconvenience to the Drinker, for the Excise officer was to survey it before any could be sold, and was not to survey it above once or twice a day'.

Interior of a London coffee house, c.1700. The proprietress and a potboy are exchanging wine glasses and cups, while another potboy dispenses tea or coffee from a tall pot. Other pots are set in front of the fire, with a cauldron for boiling water. Customers indulge in smoking, reading and politicking – the theme of this coloured engraving is probably an allusion to the Stuart cause, as represented by the portrait of the exiled James II on the wall.

The government quickly realised these new imports were desired by the fashionable and therefore slapped a hefty tax on coffee, chocolate and tea. Two Acts of Parliament passed in 1660 stipulated:

For every gallon of Coffee made and sold, to be paid by the makers thereof four pence.

For every gallon of Chocolate, Sherbert, and Tea made and sold, to be paid by the makers thereof eight pence.

So, the drinks on the menu of these colourful and exotic establishments were by no means cheap.

As well as offering the drink, coffee-house owners sold tea as dry loose leaf and customers could purchase quantities to take home to their womenfolk so that they, too, might indulge in the new drink in the comfort of their own homes. Indeed, women were not permitted to enter the coffee houses, nor probably would they have wanted to – the smell, smoke, noise, and the general maleness of the company would not have appealed. Muralt's comments would have quickly put them off. Having praised coffee houses as successful centres for business, he added, 'In other respects, they are loathsome, full of smoke like a guard-room, and as much crowded. I believe 'tis these coffee-houses that furnish the inhabitants of this great city with slander, for one hears exact accounts of everything done in town as if it were but a village.'

In 1660 Thomas Garway, London's first tea dealer, attempted to increase sales despite the high price. In a broadsheet, very much in the style of the day, he publicised tea as a healthy and beneficial drink. *An Exact Description of the Growth, Quality and Vertues of the Leaf TEA*, declared:

that the Vertues and Excellencies of this Leaf and Drink are many and great, is evident and manifest by the high esteem and use of it (especially of late years) among the physitians and knowing men in France, Italy, Holland and other parts of Christendom.

A poem published in 1685 urged a reduction in the use of alcohol. *Rebellions Antidote or a Dialogue between Coffee and Tea* included these lines:

Coffee:
The Rage and Madness of the Nation
Moves both my Heart and eke
Compassion,
...

A nineteenth-century engraving of Thomas Garway's coffee house in Exchange Alley, between Lombard Street and Cornhill in the City of London. The name was altered to Garraway's during the eighteenth century. A blue plaque on the wall marks the location of the original shop.

'Tis Wine and Ale and eke the Grape
Has Spawn'd this spurious bestial Rape;
What is't but these produce what horrid
Fact
But Wine and Ale and beer will act;
...
Tea:
Come frantick Fools leave off your
Drunken fits,
Obsequiens be and I'll recall your wits,
From perfect Madness to a modest Strain,
For Farthings four I'll fetch you back again.
Enoble all your mene with tricks of State
Enter and Sip and then attend your fate;

Come Drunk or Sober for a gentle Fee,
Come n'er so Mad, I'll your Physician be

Above: Thomas Garway's 1660 broadsheet with its fourteen clauses extolling tea's health benefits. Gravel was kidney stones or difficulty in passing urine. Lipitude distillations were the typical symptoms of a cold: runny nose, eyes, and catarrh. An ague was an acute, violent or malarial fever.

Below: As the tea trade slowly increased, more advertisements began to appear, as in this 1695 issue of A Collection for the Improvement of Husbandry & Trade. *By 1700, the East India Company was importing approximately 90,000 pounds of tea annually.*

An Exact Description of the Growth, Quality and Vertues of the Leaf TEA.

BY

Thomas Garway in Exchange-Alley near the Royal Exchange in London, Tobacconist, and Seller and Retailer of TEA and COFFEE.

TEA is generally brought from China, and groweth thereupon little Shrubs or Bushes, the Branches whereof are well garnished with white Flowers that are yellow within, of the bigness and fashion of sweet Brier, but in smell unlike, bearing thin green leaves about the bigness of Scordium, Mirtle, or Sumack, and is judged to be a kind of Sumack: This Plant hath been reported to grow wild only, but doth not, for they plant it in their Gardens about four foot distance, and it groweth about four foot high, and of the Seeds they maintain and increase their Stock. Of all places in China this Plant groweth in greatest plenty in the Province of Xemsi Latitude 36. degrees, bordering upon the West of the Province of Honam, and in the Province of Nanking near the City of Luchen, there is likewise of the growth of Sinam, Cochin-China, the Island, de Ladrones and Japan, and is called Cha. Of this famous Leaf there are divers sorts (though all of one shape) some much better than other, the upper Leaves excelling the other in fineness, a property almost in all Plants, which Leaves they gather every day, and drying them in the shade, or in Iron pans over a gentle fire till the humidity be exhausted, then put up close in Leaden pots, preserve them for their Drink Tea, which is used at Meals, and upon all Visits and Entertainments in private Families, and in the Palaces of Grandees: And it is averred by a Padre of Macao Native of Japan, that the best Tea ought not to be gathered but by Virgins who are destined to this work, and such, Quænondum Menstrua patiuntur: gemmæ quæ nascuntur in summitate arbuscula vervantur Imperatoriæ, as præcipuis ejus Dynastiis; quæ autem infra nascuntur, ad latera, populo conceduntur. The said Leaf is of such known vertues, that those very Nations so famous for Antiquity, Knowledge and Wisdom, do frequently sell it among themselves for twice its weight in Silver, and the high estimation of the Drink made therewith hath occasioned an inquiry into the nature thereof among the most intelligent persons of all Nations that have travelled in those parts, who after exact Tryal and Experience by all wayes imaginable, have commended it to the use of their several Countries, for its Vertues and Operations, particularly as followeth, viz.

The Quality is moderately hot, proper for Winter or Summer.

The Drink is declared to be most wholesome, preserving in perfect health untill extreme Old Age.

The particular Vertues are these.

It maketh the Body active and lusty.
It helpeth the Head-ach, giddiness and heaviness thereof.
It removeth the Obstructions of the Spleen.
It is very good against the Stone and Gravel, cleansing the Kidneys and Uriters being drank with Virgins Honey instead of Sugar.
It taketh away the difficulty of breathing, opening Obstructions.
It is good against Lipitude Distillations, and cleareth the Sight.
It removeth Lassitude, and cleanseth and purifieth adust Humors and a hot Liver.
It is good against Crudities, strengthening the weakness of the Ventricle or Stomach, causing good Appetite and Digestion, and particularly for Men of a corpulent Body, and such as are great eaters of Flesh.
It vanquisheth heavy Dreams, easeth the Brain, and strengtheneth the Memory.
It overcometh superfluous Sleep, and prevents Sleepiness in general, a draught of the Infusion being taken, so that without trouble whole nights may be spent in study without hurt to the Body, in that it moderately heateth and bindeth the mouth of the Stomach.
It prevents and cures Agues, Surfets and Feavers, by infusing a fit quantity of the Leaf, thereby provoking a most gentle Vomit and breathing of the Pores, and hath been given with wonderful success.
It (being prepared and drank with Milk and Water) strengtheneth the inward parts, and prevents Consumptions, and powerfully asswageth the pains of the Bowels, or griping of the Guts and Looseness.
It is good for Colds, Dropsies and Scurveys, if properly infused, purging the Blood by Sweat and Urine, and expelleth Infection.
It drives away all pains in the Collick proceeding from Wind, and purgeth safely the Gall.
And that the Vertues and Excellencies of this Leaf and Drink are many and great, is evident and manifest by the high esteem and use of it (especially of late years) among the Physitians and knowing men in France, Italy, Holland and other parts of Christendom: and in England it hath been sold in the Leaf for six pounds, and sometimes for ten pounds the pound weight, and in respect of its former scarceness and dearness, it hath been only used as a Regalia in high Treatments and Entertainments, and Presents made thereof to Princes and Grandees till the year 1657. The said Thomas Garway did purchase a quantity thereof, and first publickly sold the said Tea in Leaf and Drink, made according to the directions of the most knowing Merchants and Travellers into those Eastern Countries: And upon knowledge and experience of the said Garway's continued care and industry in obtaining the best Tea, and making Drink thereof, very many Noblemen, Physitians, Merchants and Gentlemen of Quality have ever since sent to him for the said Leaf, and daily resort to his House in Exchange-Alley aforesaid to drink the Drink thereof.
And that Ignorance nor Envy may have no ground or power to report or suggest that what is here asserted of the Vertues and Excellencies of this precious Leaf and Drink hath more of design than truth, for the justification of himself and satisfaction of others, he hath here innumerated several Authors, who in their Learned Works have expresly written and asserted the same, and much more in honour of this noble Leaf and Drink, viz. Bontius, Riccius, Jarricus, Almeyda, Horstius, Alvarez Semedo, Martinious in his China Atlas, and Alexander de Rhodes in his Voyage and Missions in a large discourse of the ordering of this Leaf, and the many Vertues of the Drink, printed at at Paris 1653. part. 10. Chap. 13.
And to the end that all Persons of Eminency and Quality, Gentlemen and others, who have occasion for Tea in Leaf may be supplyed, These are to give notice, that the said Thomas Garway hath Tea to sell from sixteen to fifty Shillings the pound.
And whereas several Persons using Coffee, have been accustomed to buy the powder thereof by the pound, or in lesser or greater quantities, which if kept two dayes looseth much of its first Goodness. And forasmuch as the Berries after drying may be kept if need require some Moneths; Therefore all persons living remote from London, and have occasion for the said powder, are advised to buy the said Coffee Berries ready dryed; which being in a Morter beaten, or in a Mill ground to powder, as they use it, will so often be brisk, fresh, and fragrant, and in its full vigour and strength as if new prepared, to the great satisfaction of the Drinkers thereof, as hath been experienced by many in this City. Which Commodity of the best sort, the said Thomas Garway hath always ready dryed to be sold at reasonable Rates.
Also such as will have Coffee in powder, or the Berries undryed, or Chocolata, may by the said Thomas Garway be supplied to their content: With such further Instructions and perfect Directions how to use Tea, Coffee and Chocolata, as is, or may be needful, and so as to be efficacious and operative, according to their several Vertues.

FINIS.

AT Shipton's Coffee-House by the Ditch side, near Fleet-Bridge, is to be sold good Gelly-Broth at one Peny the Dish, beginning at 4 of the Clock in the Morning, and very fine Tea.

The Duchess of Lauderdale's private closet at Ham House. In a room hung with 'Dark Mohayre bordered with flowered Silke with purple & gold fringe', the Duchess entertained her friends to tea. The japanned chairs, c.1675, are probably the 'backstools with cane bottomes' listed in the 1683 inventory. The tea-table of the same date is a composite piece: the upper section is Javanese, made to take tea sitting cross-legged; the lower section is Anglo-Dutch, added to bring it up to conventional height. The teapot is described in detail on page 30.

TEA AT HOME

If the ladies enjoyed their cups of tea in the privacy of their homes, they were only following the example set by their queen. It is said that when the Portuguese princess, Catharine of Braganza, arrived in England to marry Charles II, she brought with her a casket of tea. Since the Portuguese had been importing tea to Europe from the beginning of the seventeenth century, Catharine had grown up drinking tea as the preferred everyday beverage. Her fondness quickly made it fashionable in England, and first the ladies of the court and gradually those further removed from royal life developed a liking for the elegant drink. Agnes Strickland in her *Lives of the Queens of England*, published in the 1840s, pictured Catharine of Braganza's first encounter with the English royal family:

the Duchess of York came from London in her barge, to offer her homage to her royal sister-in-law. When she landed, king Charles received her at the garden gate by the waterside, and leading her by the hand, conducted her to the queen, who received her in her chamber. The duchess offered to kiss her hand, but the queen prevented her, by raising her in her arms and saluting her. The royal family then seated themselves near the queen's bed, and conversed with her. It is probable that they then partook of Catharine's favourite beverage, tea, which became a fashionable refreshment in England soon after her marriage with Charles II, though not exactly introduced by her.

When tea was consumed in such grand surroundings, it was generally within a lady's closet or bedchamber and for a mainly female gathering. The tea itself and the delicate pieces of porcelain for brewing and drinking it were displayed in the closet, and inventories for wealthy households during the seventeenth and eighteenth centuries list tea equipage not in kitchens or dining rooms but in these small private closets or boudoirs.

On the River Thames, just west of London, the Duchess of Lauderdale lived in splendour at Ham House. Married to one of the king's leading ministers, she had the finances that enabled her to purchase the latest fashions. The diarist John Evelyn described the house as 'furnished like a great Prince's with tapestries, damask, velvet, mohair on walls, bedsteads, chairs upholstered in luxurious fabrics'. By 1679, her 'white closet', a small room close to her bedchamber where she received visitors, contained 'one scriptore of princewood garnish'd wt silver, one little cedar table, six arme chayres Japand [lacquered in the Japanese manner], with black cane bottomes, one Indian furnace for tee garnished with silver'. Her more private closet was similarly furnished, with 'six Japan'd backstools with cane bottomes', a 'Japan box for sweetmeats and tea' and 'a Tea table carv'd and guilt' (see page 37). The fact that the lacquered 'backstools' had decoration on their backs suggests that they were not positioned against the walls but arranged in the middle of the room around the small lacquered table where the Duchess brewed tea with water from her silver 'Indian furnace' (see page 30) and served it to her close friends.

Lady Alice Brownlow of Belton House in Lincolnshire was left a widow when her husband died in 1697. Not only did she have the Belton estate to cope with, but five daughters for whom to find suitable husbands. She ruled the household with a rod of iron, and family tradition tells of how her daughters were once enjoying a surreptitious tea-party in one of their rooms when the dreaded footsteps could be heard approaching. To save detection, the whole tea equipage – worth a great deal of money – was promptly thrown out of the window.

A corner chimneypiece in the south-west closet at Beningbrough Hall, Yorkshire. It has been decorated in the traditional late seventeenth-century manner with 'famille verte' Chinese Kangxi porcelain, including three teapots. Daniel Defoe suggested that it was Queen Mary II's penchant for Chinese blue and white porcelain that set the fashion for oriental ceramics, but their popularity was also as a result of the imports brought to England by the East India Company.

Family records and household accounts for members of the upper classes show a very gradual increase in the consumption of tea through the last part of the seventeenth century. In 1673, Lord Roos' steward recorded buying 'a box of tin to keepe his lordship's tea in coole'. In 1685, the 1st Duke of Bedford's daughter, Lady Margaret Russell, received a set of tea dishes bought by her father's steward for £1 14s 0d. In 1688, the steward purchased a tea salver for 5 shillings and, in 1689 or 1690, a teapot for £2 3s 0d. Like Lady Alice Brownlow of Belton, Margaret Bankes was a formidable chatelaine. When she married John Bankes of Kingston Hall (now Kingston Lacy) in Dorset in 1691, the estate was in a bad way financially. She brought much-needed money, bore Bankes ten children, and kept her accounts meticulously so that we are able to follow the arrival of tea in the household and the purchase of increasingly sophisticated tea ware and tea furniture. In July 1693 Margaret 'Pay'd for a red china teapot 10/-, for 6 tea dishes and a sugar box 12/', and in August, she also bought a brown earthen teapot for 2/6. In that same year she started to buy tea equipage: in January 'a black Japan table for my closet £1. 15. 0' (see page 37), and in July, 'a tin sugar box, tea box & 2 saucepans 4/-'. The first mention of tea itself in her accounts appears in 1706

when she bought 'a pound of green tea £1.1.0.' In July 1713 she bought 'a pound of imperial tea £1.6s.0, a pound of Bohea tea £1.5. 0', and in December 'a quarter of a pound of green tea 4/6'.

Living away from London could have provided a hindrance to the growth in the consumption of tea. Lady Grisell Baillie, living in Edinburgh, had to rely upon her husband's visits to London on business to provide her with small and infrequent amounts of tea, both black and green. Only in 1708 do regular purchases of tea by the lady herself begin to feature in the household accounts. The account book of Sarah Fell, one of seven step-daughters of the Quaker George Fox, shows the regular pattern of acquiring supplies for their home at Swarthmoor Hall in Lancashire between 1673 and 1678. Basic goods were bought locally on market days but major supplies had to be transported from Lancaster, Kendal and Kirby Lonsdale – journeys that presented all sorts of hazards. From London came supplies of sugar, oranges and fancy articles such as gloves, but there is no mention of tea.

The absence of tea from most household account books for the late seventeenth century may not be entirely due to a complete ignorance outside London of its existence or a lack of interest in drinking it. It may simply be

that tea was such an expensive item that supplies were not bought as part of the list of everyday requirements, but were acquired separately by a superior member of the household staff or by a family member, and the expenditure noted elsewhere in accounts that have not survived. The first bill for tea in the records of the Dukes of Bedford at Woburn dates from 1685 when just over £10 was paid. In 1687, nearly £15 was spent on one kind of tea that cost 3 guineas per pound and another that cost 25 shillings, and several smaller bills in 1692 show tea costing 3 guineas a pound. But these bills are not amongst the everyday accounts. They are among the steward's separate papers and show that it was Mr Dawson, the assistant to the Receiver General and a very high-ranking member of staff in the hierarchy, who was responsible for buying the tea. Sometimes the task fell to his wife, who often travelled from Bedfordshire to the family's London home, Bedford House in the Strand, in order to help the housekeeper there. While in town, she sometimes made the necessary journey up the road to the City to the premises of a certain Mr Richards from whom the tea was purchased. The household steward, who kept a careful record of moneys spent on tea and coffee, also played a part in acquiring the tea. It had always been his responsibility to make regular trips to the London wharves to collect and pay for such foreign delicacies as hams from Germany, fish from Newfoundland and fruit from the East Indies and China. In time, his shopping list came to include tea that came in from Holland and cost £1 16s 0d per pound. Once he had found what he wanted, he would pay for it, pay the customs due and arrange for its delivery to Bedford House.

Garway announced in his broadsheet of 1660 that 'the said Thomas Garway hath Tea to sell from, sixteen to sixty shillings the pound' and 'that all Persons of Emminency and Quality, Gentlemen and others, who have occasion for Tea in Leaf may be supplied'. The small amounts of tea consumed in private houses in the seventeenth century were not only purchased from general merchants like Garway or the Bedfords' Mr Richards, but also from apothecaries who traded in remedies and medicinal herbs, reinforcing the idea that tea was a health-giving tonic. The Duke of Bedford's household also purchased tea from Elmes Foster, a druggist in Bedford Street who sold coffee, tea, chocolate, sago, hartshorn, snuff 'and all sorts of drugs', and from William Robinson at The Greyhound & King's Arms in Fleet Street.

A Tea Party *by the Dutch artist, Nicolaes Verkolje (1673–1746). This is one of the earliest depictions of tea drinking, and shows a selection of Chinese porcelain, including small tea bowls and saucers, arranged for the party. The large bowl in the centre of the table is for slops, the two small dishes for sugar and bread and butter. The tiny redware teapot is Chinese, from Yixing, while the silver kettle and teaspoons are probably English.*

TEA AND MEALTIMES

In the early seventeenth century, the first meal of the day for the wealthy consisted of cold meats and fish, cheeses and ale or beer taken at six or seven o'clock in the morning. The less privileged breakfasted on a pint of old ale, a cup of sack or a home-made syrup of herbs, spices and alcohol, and a little bread, while the poor consumed a mug of ale and a bowlful of pottage (a soupy porridge) made from whatever grains and cereals were available.

By the end of the century, tea drinking was slowly becoming a part of everyday life for most wealthy families. The breakfast table in a few noble households was now arranged with platefuls of buttered bread or toast, and pots of tea, coffee or chocolate. Poorer families, and those living in more distant parts of Britain, were still not familiar with these expensive beverages and continued to drink ale, beer, whisky, and home-made cordials and syrups with their daily meals.

In the early 1600s, the main meal of the day was eaten at some time between eleven o'clock and noon, but as the century wore on, the time for dinner grew gradually later. The dining table of the prosperous was laden with joints of roast meats and dishes of offal and fish.

On 26 January 1660, Samual Pepys recorded that his wife had prepared 'a very fine dinner – viz. A dish of marrow bones, a leg of mutton, a loin of veal, a dish of fowl, three pullets, and two dozen of larks all in a dish; a great tart, a neat's [ox] tongue, a dish of anchovies, a dish of prawns and cheese. My company was my father, my uncle Fenner, his two sons, Mr Pierce, and all their wives, and my brother Tom.'

These mealtimes were often very alcoholic affairs. Before the arrival of tea and coffee, the staple drink for most people throughout the day was beer or ale. For those that could afford them, imported wines and spirits were taken at mealtimes, and in Scotland, whisky became more and more popular as the industry grew. But the drink of the masses was home-brewed or locally produced ales made from barley, or beers made from hops.

In 1686, Dr Giovanni Gemelli-Careri in his *Travels through Europe* wrote of the English, 'They fill themselves extravagantly with several sorts of liquor, as beer and ale, aqua vitae, perry [from the fermented juice of pears], mead, cider, mum, and usquebaugh [whisky], a violent burning drink.' It was not unusual for men to drink themselves into a coma and end up on the floor under the dining table.

The day ended for most people with a light supper which was eaten between 5pm and 8pm, depending on family and work routines, and varied from cold meats, cheese and bread for the wealthy to more pottage or porridge, oatcakes or bread for the poor.

A detail from Francis Sandford's History of the Coronation of James II, *published in London in 1687. The dishes for one course of the feast have been laid out in groups so that the peers and their consorts can help themselves to a selection. Drinks are taken from a court cupboard at the top of the picture, and served to the guests on request – glasses and bottles do not stand on the dining tables.*

Not wishing to sit amongst tobacco smoke and loud drunken masculine conversation, the ladies would withdraw to a closet or withdrawing room as soon as dinner was finished. Here they would indulge in the more demure occupations of needlework and light conversation.
It is at this point in England's history that Catharine of Braganza's influence began to change attitudes to alcohol and set a pattern of behaviour for the ladies.
As Agnes Strickland wrote of the queen,

Yet, as Catharine of Braganza was certainly the first tea-drinking queen of England, she has the credit of setting the fashion for the use of that temperate beverage, in an age when ladies, as well as gentlemen, at all times of the day, heated or stupefied their brains with ale and wine, for the want of the more refined substitutes of tea, coffee and chocolate. The use of the simple luxuries had in time a beneficial influence on the manners of all classes of society, by forming a counter charm against habits of intoxication, and have promoted the progress of civilization in no slight degree.

Catharine of Braganza, the Portuguese princess who set the fashion for tea drinking in England when she married Charles II in 1662.

In 1694, William Congreve in his play, *The Double Dealer*, included a line which revealed that a different social pattern was already beginning to emerge. The ladies, one character explains, were 'at the end of the gallery, retired to their tea and scandal according to their ancient custom after dinner'.

Some gentlemen also partook of this tea-drinking ritual. Lord Clarendon wrote in his diary for 10 February 1688, 'Le Père Couplet supped with me; he is a man of very good conversation. After supper we had tea, which he said was as good as any he had drank in China. The Chinese who came over with him and Mr Fraser, supped likewise with us.' And Lord Keeper Guildford, who died in 1685, was accustomed to offering tea to visitors and when entertaining 'the nobility and gentry coming to London, gave them a solemn service of tea in the withdrawing room, after which the company usually left'.

But Henry Savile did not approve of all this tea drinking. In a letter to his uncle, Mr Secretary Coventry of His Majesty's Government, he complained about his friends 'who call for tea, instead of pipes and bottles after dinner, a base unworthy Indian practise, and which I must ever admire your most Christian family for not admitting'.

In 1673–4 the Duke and Duchess of Lauderdale prepared a magnificent apartment at Ham House for a visit by Charles II's queen, Catharine of Braganza. This is the closet, where she could withdraw from the formality of the state rooms. The gilt armchair in the alcove is a 'sleeping chayre' with an adjustable back for 'reposeing': with a cup of tea?

A Dehua teapot of the Kangxi period, from the third quarter of the seventeenth century, now in the Duchess of Lauderdale's private closet at Ham House. Dehua refers to the kilns in which these pieces were made, producing a colourless glaze that allows the pure white of the porcelain to show. It is decorated with mounts of European silver-gilt of the same period.

EARLY TEA RITUALS

When tea was drunk at home, servants brought all the necessary equipage to the appropriate room. It was the lady (or gentleman) of the house, however, who actually brewed and served the tea to guests and family. Since tea was prepared in the room where it was to be drunk, a servant would bring in the crucial supply of boiling water at the relevant moment, and pour it into an appropriate vessel. Tea kettles, known also as furnaces, appeared towards the end of the century. The Duchess of Lauderdale, as ever in the vanguard of fashion, had an 'Indian furnace for tee' in her closet at Ham House as early as the 1670s. The Bankes family at Kingston Hall purchased a 'tea frame & kettle' for £2 0s 0d in 1693. In Edinburgh in 1696, Lady Grisell Baillie's mother-in-law owned a 'whet ern tea stop' (a white iron tea stoup or container for water).

The precious green or black tea leaves were stored in Chinese porcelain jars kept on the shelves of the closet. These jars, small and round, or tall and flat-sided, had little pull-off caps that were used as a measure, and were decorated with the same delicate motifs that appeared on the porcelain teapots and bowls. The word 'caddy' did not come into use until the end of the eighteenth century.

A silver tea kettle with its stand, made by the London silversmith, Thomas Sadler in 1712. It is decorated with the arms of Edward Dryden impaling those of his wife Elizabeth Allen, and stands in the dining room of their home, Canons Ashby in Northamptonshire.

The tea was measured carefully into a small Chinese teapot. These teapots arrived in London on the same ships as the tea, and were purchased from a tea dealer or a porcelain merchant. The dainty pots had evolved at the time when the fashion for whipping powdered tea into a bowlful of hot water gave way to a preference for infused tea made from large pieces of leaf. Needing a vessel in which to steep the leaves, the Chinese adapted the traditional water or wine ewer to tea brewing. The area most famous for the manufacture of teapots was (and still is) Yixing in Jiangsu Province, where the special rich red stoneware clay is thought to create a pot that best draws out the flavour of the tea. It was these little unglazed pots, often made in fanciful shapes and designs, that first appeared on English tea-tables from the 1660s onwards.

After them came glazed porcelain pots like those used at the Imperial Chinese court, decorated with delicate images of flowers, butterflies, birds and Chinese figures. The pots were small not because, as has sometimes been suggested, tea was so expensive, but because that was how the Chinese made them for their own use. European traders were not placing commissions for specific pieces at this time, but were simply buying and shipping whatever goods were available in both Japan and China. When they arrived in London, people snapped them up.

Once the tea had steeped for a few minutes, it was poured into small handleless Chinese porcelain bowls that held anything from two or three elegantly sipped mouthfuls to two or three tablespoons. The saucers were shallow. It is said that the idea of the saucer developed in the seventh century AD when the daughter of a Chinese military official found it difficult to handle the hot bowls of tea she brewed for him and asked a local potter to devise a little plate on which to place the bowl.

Paintings of European families at tea during the seventeenth century mostly show tables arranged with kettle, teapot, tea canister, dishes and saucers of porcelain, a basin for the slops, a bowl or dish of sugar, little spoons for stirring the sugar into the tea, and sometimes a dish upon which to rest them when not in use. The use of sugar in tea followed the normal practice of adding sweeteners to herbal brews of flowers, leaves and seeds for tonic drinks to make them more palatable. Tea was, after all, sold as a herb with medicinal qualities. Samuel Pepys noted in his diary for 28 June 1667 that he arrived home and 'there find my wife making of Tea, a drink which Mr Pelling, the pothecary tells her is good for her cold and defluxions [runny nose and eyes]'. Housewives were expected to be skilled in concocting brews for different illnesses and almost always added sugar or honey as sweeteners. So, right from the earliest days of tea drinking in England, sugar was commonly added and stirred in with little silver spoons.

Until the sixteenth century, sugar was imported from Brazil, the Azores and the Canary Islands at great expense, but when supplies of sugar began to come from the West Indies the price was brought down by half. Figures for 1660 show sugar consumption to be an average of approximately 2lb per person per year. By the end of the century, this figure had doubled, and the increase may well have been caused by an increased consumption of tea and coffee as well as the wider use of sugar generally in sweetmeats and desserts.

Not everybody thought that this heavy use of sugar in tea was reasonable. John Ovington wrote, 'Yet some will urge that although these Virtues which I have mention'd may be fairly attributed to this China Liquor, yet are they sometimes obstructed by the use of that Sugar which is commonly mix'd with it. And this indeed, I must confess, may somewhat abate the Efficacy of it in some Operations; yet this Advantage it produces, in benefiting of the Lungs and Reins [kidneys]; to which it is a mighty Friend.'

Two pieces of tea ware in slip-cast red stoneware. The teapot was probably made by J.& D.Elers of Staffordshire, c.1695, produced in imitation of oriental imports and carrying a pseudo-Chinese mark. The tea canister was made in Yixing, south-east China, c.1690. It is decorated with a sacred dragon, lizard and pheasants. The lid has a gated locking mechanism to prevent pilfering of the expensive contents.

Until the end of the seventeenth century, it was rare to add milk to the little bowls of tea. Milk or cream jugs made their appearance in paintings only in the late seventeenth and early eighteenth centuries, when the use of milk in tea slowly became fashionable. In 1698, Rachel, Lady Russell, wrote to her daughter to report that 'yesterday, I met with little bottles to pour milk out for tea; they call them milk bottles. I was much delighted with them, and so put them up for a present to you.' Four years later, she made a point of saying that 'excellent green tea is good with milk'.

As well as providing an elegant digestif after dinner, tea was also occasionally used as the base for more nourishing drinks. In 1664, Sir Kenelm Digby noted down a recipe for a tea caudle that he had learned from a Jesuit priest returning from China.

To near a pint of the infusion, take two yolks of new-laid eggs, and beat them very well with as much fine sugar as is sufficient for this quantity of liquor; when they are very well incorporated, pour your tea upon the eggs and sugar, and stir them well together. So drink it hot. This is when you come home from attending business abroad, and are very hungry, and yet have not conveniency to eat presently a competent meal.

But he warned that:

in these parts we let the hot water remain too long soaking upon the tea, which maketh it extract into it self the earthly parts of the herb. The water is to remain upon [the tea] no longer than whilst you can say the Miserere psalm very leisurely…. Thus you have only the spiritual parts of the Tea, which is much more active, penetrative and friendly to nature. (You may for this regard take a little more of the herb; about one dragm of Tea will serve for a pint of water; which makes three ordinary draughts.)

TEA WARES AND FURNITURE

Long before the first cargoes of tea started arriving in London, the East India Company had been importing porcelains from China and Japan. As the interest in tea grew, so the company struggled to keep pace with the demand for bowls, teapots, saucers and storage jars. No European potter had discovered the secret of manufacturing such fine translucent porcelain and the oriental 'china' or 'cheyney' (also cheny, chenea, and chiney) pieces were therefore much sought after.

But it was not always easy to satisfy customers, for careless packing and a two-year voyage on rough seas meant that many of the expensive pieces arrived broken or cracked. In 1685, the Directors of the Company wrote angrily to their agent in China: 'We can now but briefly tell you that we are amazed at the prices you have invoiced to us, your own goods from Chyna, being 50 per cent as near as we can guess more than they will bring here – the Rhubarb [sic] is not worth the freight, the Thea generally trash – the thea cups dear at 1d apiece.'

Company records list the types of goods shipped out of Amoy in 1699 and their relative values:

58 nests Jappan bowls	15s 0d each
6 d⁰	8s 0d each
2,500 Jappan tea cups	6d each
2,690 saucers	
814 Jappan tea cups	1s 6d each
330 Jappan tea cups	5d each
340 d⁰ saucers	

The cargoes of tea wares and other porcelain being shipped out of China and Japan came in mixed batches, with bowls and saucers of different designs and sizes, and few people had matching sets but rather random selections of individual pieces. They were distributed in Britain by merchants who also traded tea and coffee, glassware and pottery.

An inventory made in November 1682 lists all the pieces of china that belonged to Frances Cranfield, Dowager Countess of Dorset.

MY LADYS CHENEY IN HER CHAMBER

five peices of cheyney (tipt) [decorated with gold leaf]

five peices of christolets (tipt)

two tea potts (tipt)

two greater jars of cheyny

five lesser jars of cheyny

twelve Blew tee dishes

eighteene white tee dishes

tenn wrought white cupps

six flatt white dishes

six white and Redd dishes and 1 cupp to it

six green dishes

two white tee cupps wrought

seaventeen pieces of cheyney of severall sorts

one cheyny plate, one cupp and a cheyney standish

two pomander dishes

one tee table one Indian baskett

Margaret Bankes, who had only acquired a few pieces of china ware for Kingston Hall in the 1690s, now began buying regularly. In June 1701, she paid for 'a sett of tea dishes and saucers 18/-'; in January 1702, for '6 tea dishes and sasers 10/-, for a teapot 3/6, for a kenester 3/6'. By 1713, she had bought nine teapots, more dishes and saucers, 'a china suggar dish' and a pair of tea tongs. At Dyrham Park in Gloucestershire (see page 86), William Blathwayt was acquiring a selection of oriental tea ware, listed in an inventory taken in 1710: '12 Tea Dishes, 12 fine reddish Tea Cupps, 6 Tea Cupps with little scallops upon ye Edges, 5 Tea Potts, a Tea pott & Canister, 6 China Tea pots & 1 Stone one, 2 red & gold China Sugar Boxes, 5 ribb'd blew & white Tea Dishes, 5 plain red & Gold Tea Cups, 6 red and green burnt China Tea Dishes, 6 sawcers of ye same.'

Almost as soon as tea became available, European potters had recognised the potential and started to manufacture copies of Chinese red earthenware teapots. Fulham Pottery in London was making red stoneware pots in the 1670s. And Celia Fiennes noted in her diary while travelling from Wolseley into Wales in 1698, 'I went to this Newcastle in Staffordshire to see them making the fine tea-potts cups and saucers of the fine red earth, in imitation and as curious as that which comes from China.'

Delftware was also becoming a familiar sight on British tables. It took its origins from Italian majolica, the white, tin-glazed pots and dishes with decoration in coloured enamel. When the first oriental porcelains arrived in Holland via the Portuguese in the mid-sixteenth century, Dutch potters started to copy the typical blue on white designs using their existing techniques. In the 1560s some of the most successful potters took their craft to England, where their wares were regarded as superior to anything the English were producing, and by the 1660s potteries had been established at Southwark in London, dedicated to the manufacture of popular oriental-style goods. In 1717, a group of London potters moved to Liverpool, where Delftware was produced on a large scale, decorated with the now familiar blue, red, yellow, green or purple designs of landscapes with figures, seascapes, birds, flowers and insects in the Chinese style.

European potters gradually increased their production of stoneware and earthenware teapots, but it was not until the mid-eighteenth century that they produced anything that serious rivalled the quality and beauty of the Chinese and Japanese wares (see pages 82-3). Those who could afford them still preferred the more expensive oriental pots, bowls and saucers. For those with wealth, an alternative was silver. The first recorded silver teapot was presented to the Directors of the East India Company by one of its members. It bears the inscription 'This silver tea Pott was presented to the Com[ttee] of the East India Company by the Right Hono[r] George Ld Berkeley of Berkeley Castle. A member of that Honourable and worthy Society and A true hearty Lover of them. 1670.'

Left: Dutch Delft teapots, marked 'J.Hoppesteyn' and dating from the 1670s and '80s, from the ceramic collection at Wallington in Northumberland.

Right: Silver teapot presented in 1670 by Lord Berkeley to the Committee of the East India Company. This is the first recorded teapot in silver in England, and its shape resembles that of coffee pots.

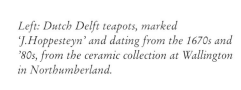

Tall and tapering with a straight spout, the pot looks very like those used to serve coffee in coffee houses, and is typical for the period. It was not until the early eighteenth century that the rounder, pear-shaped teapot became more popular. Some households even chose silver tea bowls: the Duchess of Lauderdale certainly had a set of eighteen at Ham House in 1672. Although they must have looked wonderful, they were extremely impractical since the metal would have become too hot to hold once filled with boiling tea.

Jars for leaf tea were also fashioned by English silversmiths. They copied the shape and form of the porcelain tea jars that arrived from China, often engraving them with a B for Bohea and a G for green tea. Tall and flat-sided, they sometimes had a panel in the base that slid off to allow access to the inner lead container for refilling, or alternatively an entire top section that slid off. As with the porcelain jars, the little pull-off caps were used for measuring the leaves into the teapot.

Small silver spoons for both tea and coffee were in use from the mid-seventeenth century. They were available in several different forms – wrought, with plain handles, with twisted handles or decorated with little knobs. Most were gilt and were bought in sets or individually. In 1693, Margaret Bankes purchased '6 silver double gilt tea spoons £1. 12. 0' and in 1700, 'a tea spoon 2/6'. The 1697 inventory of plate belonging to Charles Sackville, 6th Earl of Dorset at Knole lists '6 guilt Tea spoons'.

The earliest tea-tables were salvers or trays that were made to sit on top of another specially designed table. Tables with legs that were primarily made to hold tea equipage came into use at the end of the century and so many were imported from Japan and China that the London Joiners' Company got up a petition to protest. This stated that 6,582 tea-tables had been imported in the previous four years and the joiners were obviously fearful for their jobs. The Duchess of Lauderdale's private closet contained just such a tea-table 'carv'd and guilt' from Java. She had a lower stage added to bring it up to the right height for use in her home. Margaret Bankes was a little behind the Duchess in acquiring tea-tables, buying only one 'black Japan table for my closet' in 1693, but making up for it in the first ten years of the next century when she apparently bought four: in 1702, 'a hand tea table £3. 0. 0; in 1705, 'a hand tea table of wallnut tree 4/-'; in 1709, 'a little hand tea-table 3/6'; and in 1711, 'a tea table and a pair of sconces'.

In 1713, in The *Review*, Daniel Defoe noted with approval

It is impossible that Coffee, Tea and Chocolate can be so advanced in their Consumption, without an eminent Encrease of those Trades that attend them; whence we see the most noble Shops in the City taken up with the most valuable Utensils of the Tea-table.

He was right. As tea became more popular, so the trade in teapots, cups and saucers, sugar basins, milk jugs, sugar spoons and tongs grew. The East India Company, along with individual traders, were enjoying a thriving business.

'Tom's Coffee House', opened by Thomas Twining in Devereux Court on the Strand in 1706, from an early nineteenth-century watercolour. His tea and coffee house, the Golden Lyon, was established next door eleven years later.

The Eighteenth Century

TEA FOR SALE

By 1714, when George I came to the throne, the growing interest in tea had encouraged more merchants to specialise in selling it. Grocers and general merchants added it to their list of supplies, while coffee-house proprietors increased their offerings and their sales. Twining's coffee house, established in Devereux Court in the Strand in 1706, was doing so well with its sales that the family decided, in 1717, to expand into the premises at No. 217 next door. The location was ideal. The Strand was just outside the limits of the City, where there were already more than 2,000 coffee houses, but very close to the Inns of Court, so it immediately attracted barristers and attorneys from the nearby law firms. Also within the same area were the town houses of several aristocratic families and the business thus acquired an impressive list of distinguished customers, including the Earl of Powis, the Earl and Countess of Lichfield, the Duke of Somerset, the Duke of Beaufort, and the Countess of Stamford, all of whom kept not just a house in London but large country estates elsewhere in England, Scotland, Wales and Ireland. The shop also supplied tea to naval and army officers, members of the clergy, and 'the Windsor Castle Steward of all the Lordships, Manors and Lands etc', as well as a long list of grocers and coffee-house owners – some of whom had businesses as far afield as Winchester, Newbury, Chester, Shrewsbury and Devizes.

Very importantly, Twining's shop at The Golden Lyon was one of the first into which ladies could step to buy their tea. Prior to this, ladies had to send their husbands or male servants into the forbidden interior of a coffee house to purchase the loose leaf for home consumption. Now carriages drew up in the Strand and waited while aristocratic ladies dealt directly with the tea merchant. Once inside, they would buy their favourite tea straight from one of the open chests or have a blend specially made up. Richard Twining explained in 1784 that 'In my grandfather's time ... it was the custom for Ladies and Gentle-men to come to the shop, and to order

their own Teas – the chests used to be spread out, and when my grandfather had mixed some of them together, in the presence of his customers, they used to taste the Tea: and the mixing was varied till it suited the palates of the purchasers.'

Even a specialised tea merchant was prepared to expand his stock. Twining's ledgers show an interesting entry for a Mr A. Warrender of Bath as having purchased a 'set of china dishes, a diamond ring, 3 pairs of dice' at the shop some time between 1715 and 1720. Druggists, apothecaries and coffee houses were now joined in the tea trade by china and glassware merchants, milliners, mercers and goldsmiths. In 1805, for instance, a merchant by the name of Isaac James, of No. 10 Wine Street, Bristol, offered a long and varied list of goods which he advertised in a rhyming catalogue that included pictures, books, battledores, pencils, slates, copy books, grammars [hornbooks], dictionaries, ink, paper, writing desks, quills, purses, thread-cases, pocket books, wedding gloves, stationery, pills, tonics, herbs and:

Bibles, and Prayer books, Preparations,
Hymn-books, for different Persuasions.
These you may muse upon at Tea;
You can't buy better than of me,
Both Black and Green, in printed papers,
Most excellent against the vapours.

Portrait of Thomas Twining, founder of the tea and coffee business. He was determined to sell only tea of the very best quality, a philosophy that earned him the respect and loyalty of many wealthy and aristocratic clients.

For the first 30 years of the eighteenth century, prices remained high, mainly due to a 14 per cent duty on all teas imported by the East India Company, and a further fluctuating excise tax of approximately 5 shillings per pound. The beverage therefore retained its image as an expensive and exotic luxury to be enjoyed only by the wealthy. In 1723, the excise tax was reduced to 4 shillings and, in 1745, a reduction to 1 shilling caused a considerable drop in prices. The effect

Twining's eighteenth-century business card from the company's shop at No. 216 the Strand.

was almost instantaneous. Home consumption rose rapidly from 800,000lb weight in the five-year period from 1741 to 1745 to more than 2,500,000lb from 1746 to 1750. The amount consumed continued to reflect the level of taxation. In 1784, the total import duty and excise on a pound of tea amounted to a tax of 119 per cent, and in that year, the British drank almost 5 million lb of tea. When the 1784 Tea and Window Act cut the tea tax to 12 per cent, consumption rose to almost 11 million lb in one year, and not far short of 12,500,000lb in two.

Household accounts reflect this trend by showing how gradually larger quantities were being purchased more frequently. At Petworth House, the Sussex home of the Wyndham family, an invoice shows that in November 1750, 4lb of fine Hyson were bought from merchants Edward and Sarah Schellinger for 16 shillings a pound, whereas the same would have cost £1 or more in 1720. On 5 March 1759, the family purchased 2lb of fine Hyson, and on 17 March, a further 4lb of tea was bought from 'Twinings & Carter in Devereux Court near Temple Bar, London'. Throughout the century, Petworth House continued to buy its supplies from a number of merchants, including Daniel Twining, the Schellingers, Twining and Carter, John Brownhill, and William Umpleby –

all tea dealers – and from Thomas Morgan, china dealer, and Thomas Wells, grocer, tea and coffee merchant.

In the 1750s, the 4th Duke of Bedford was buying regular orders of '2 pounds fine Green Tea', (at 12s per pound) and '2 pounds fine Congo Tea' (at 10s per pound) from 'Richard Haines, Chocolate-maker, at Tom's Coffee House, Covent Garden, who sells Superfine Vanilla and Plain Carracca Chocolate, Finest Teas of all Sorts, best High Roasted Turkey-Coffee, Spanish Havannah, etc., Snuffs, Wholesale and Retail, at Reasonable Rates'. At Saltram House in Devon, Mr Parker's account book for 1780 noted, 'By cash to Mr Simmonds for tea, nineteen pounds, twelve shillings. To Bradley for tea, fifteen pounds, seven shillings'. And in the 1770s at Stourhead in Wiltshire, Sir Richard Hoare was buying fine Souchong, fine green and quantities of unspecified tea three times a month, along with loaf sugar and canisters for the tea which he then had engraved.

By the early nineteenth century, in Cockermouth in Cumberland, Dorothy Wordsworth was ordering considerable amounts of tea to be shipped to her by canal. On 25 October 1828 she ordered '6lb of good West India coffee (roasted), 75lb of Souchong tea and 30lb of Congou.'

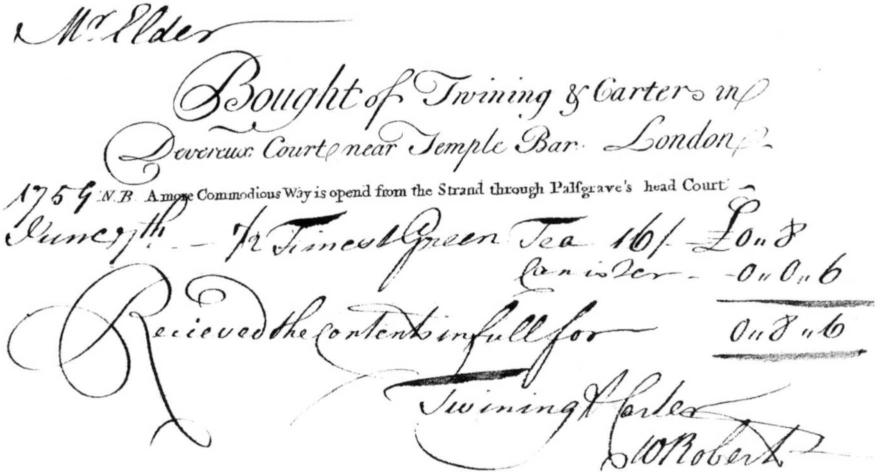

Mr Elder

Bought of Twining & Carter in

Devereux Court near Temple Bar London

1759 N.B. A more Commodious Way is opend from the Strand through Palfgrave's head Court

June 9th — 1/2 Finest Green Tea 16/ £0 .. 8

Canister — 0 .. 0 .. 6

Recieved the contents in full for — 0 .. 8 .. 6

Twining & Carter

W Robert

Tho.s Elder Esq.r

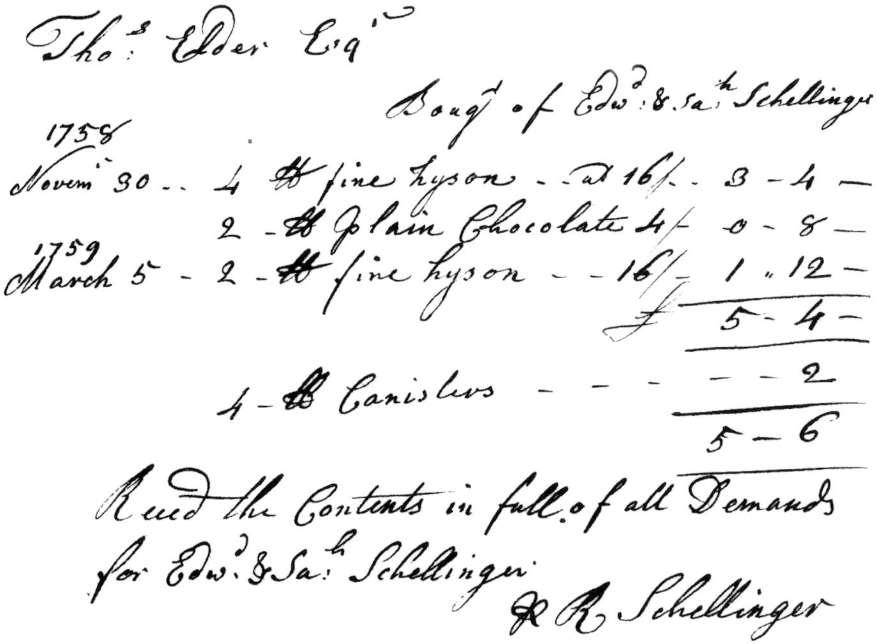

Bough of Edw.d & Sa.h Schellinger

1758					
Novem.r 30 ..	4 ℔ fine hyson	at 16/	3 — 4 —		
	2 — ℔ plain Chocolate 4/		0 — 8 —		
1759					
March 5 -	2 — ℔ fine hyson — 16/		1 .. 12 —		
			5 — 4 —		
4 — ℔ Canisters — — — —			— — 2		
			5 — 6		

Reced the Contents in full. of all Demands
for Edw.d & Sa.h Schellinger

R Schellinger

*Two household bills from Petworth House,
showing Thomas Elder's purchases of tea for the
Wyndham family; from Twinings & Carter,
1759, and from the Schellingers, 1758 and 1759.*

ILLICIT TEA

Tea, like spirits, silk, jewellery and tobacco, was desired by consumers but liable to heavy tax and duty. It was thus a commodity destined to attract the attention of smugglers. A complex network of smuggling brought untaxed supplies into Britain from the East Indies, India, China and Japan, often via Holland or France. Fishermen's boots were filled with gloves and jewellery, ladies' petticoats were padded out with lace and silk stockings, hollow loaves of bread concealed amber and more lace, sailcloth was furled around tobacco and rolls of silk.

Tea, originating mostly from the Dutch East Indies, was landed along the south coast of England, divided up and wrapped in oilskin bags ready to be loaded on to pack horses and carts. If no immediate transport was available, it was concealed under hedges and bushes to await later collection. In 1778, Edward Giddy of Tredrea in Cornwall wrote to the Chief Customs Officer: 'Smuggling, since the soldiers have been drawn off,

Thomas Rowlandson's cartoon 'Rigging out a Smuggler', published by Thomas Tegg in 1810. This shows the practice of concealing contraband around the person: the comely lady has a barrel of cognac and panniers of tea, and a bottle of perfume wedged firmly between her breasts.

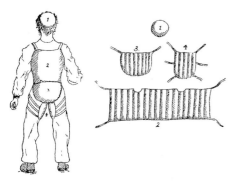

METHODS OF SMUGGLING TEA. — III.

1, Cotton bag to fit crown of hat ; 2, Cotton stays or waistcoat ; 3, Bustle for lower part of back ; 4, Thigh pieces. N.B.—The whole contained 30 lbs of tea.

Drawings from Henry Shore's Smuggling Days and Smuggling Ways *showing ingenious methods for hiding tea. Smugglers earned 20 shillings or more per night while carriers and riders could expect 5 shillings. Each man was also allowed a 'dollop' of tea – 40 pounds weight, worth about 25 shillings.*

has been carried on almost without control. ... About a fortnight since, a large wherry landed ... fifteen hundred to two thousand ankers [a measure, formerly used in England and on the Continent, equivalent to 10 old wine gallons or 8⅓ imperial gallons] of spirits, about twenty tons of tea, and other kinds of smuggled goods.'

The amounts of contraband goods were huge. A House of Commons return stated that between 1822 and 1824 officials had seized '129 vessels, 746 boats; 135,000 gallons of brandy, 227,000 gallons of gin; 10,500 gallons of whisky,

253 gallons rum; 3,000lbs snuff; 19,000lbs of tea; 42,000 yards of silk'. Of these, it was tea and 'foreign spirits' that led the field. A nineteenth-century report of the *Commission of Excise on Smuggling* estimated that the excise duties lost on these amounted annually to £950,000. The smuggled tea sold for between 5s and 7s per pound, whereas the official price stood at anything from 10 shillings to £1 6s 0d per pound. Given that the average weekly wage of an unskilled workman was approximately 10 shillings, it is no wonder that the black market thrived.

The illicit trade encompassed not just criminals and petty thieves but respected members of society who, even if not actually involved in the smuggling, concealing and distribution of the tea, certainly bought the untaxed leaf. The Rev. James Woodforde recorded in his diary for 16 January 1777 that he had given 'To one Richard Andrews a smuggler for a pound of 9/- Tea, and 3 Silk India Handkerchiefs at 5/6 – £1. 5. 6.' And on 29 March that same year, 'Andrews the smuggler brought me this night about 11 o'clock a bagg of Hyson Tea 6 pd weight. He frightened us a little by whistling under the Parlour Window just as we were going to bed. I gave him some Geneva [gin] and paid him for the tea at 10/6 per pd £3. 3. 0.'

In his *Observations on the Tea & Window Act and on the Tea Trade*, 1785, Richard Twining commented that 'the smuggler has become so formidable a rival [to the East India Company], that, upon the most moderate computation, they shared the Tea-trade equally between them; and according to some calculations, the smuggler had two thirds of it.'

Smuggling continued well into the nineteenth century, as Henry Shore explained in *Smuggling Days and Smuggling Ways*:

During the year 1831, an extensive system of smuggling tea was discovered to be carried on from Havre de Grace, the cargoes being generally run in the Thames, at the back of the Isle of Wight, and on the Hampshire coast. The tea was packed in cases made to fit between the timbers of vessels, so as to resemble flooring. A few years later, in 1833, another method was discovered by means of which tea and dry goods were often brought into the country, viz., inside of a cape, or suspended from the shoulders under a great-coat, or under petticoat trousers, such as were used by fishermen and pilots.... In 1835, a curious device was discovered to be in use amongst Deal boatmen, concealed under their tarpaulin jackets and trousers.

THE TEAS ON OFFER

By 1800, the tea trade had really burgeoned. Robert Wisset summed up its progress in *A View of the rise, progress and present state of the Tea Trade in Europe*: 'Tea at the beginning of the last century was scarcely known as a commodity of traffic: it now holds the most distinguished rank in the list of Asiatic imports.'

Consumers still selected from 20 or so different varieties. Twinings offered the following:

	Wholesale	*Retail*
Bohea	*12/- to 21/-*	*16/- to 24/-*
Bohea Dust	*8/- to 12/-*	*12/- to 16/-*
Bohea with Pekoe	*27/- to 18/-*	*20/- to 24/-*
Pekoe	*18/- to 20/-*	*24/- to 30/-*
Imperial	*18/- to 26/-*	*20/- to 30/-*
Bloom & Imperial	*16/- to 20/-*	*18/- to 24/-*
Congo	*18/- to 20/-*	*20/- to 30/-*
Congo with Pekoe	*20/-*	*22/- to 30/-*
Congo with Bohea	*18/- to 20/-*	*18/- to 22/-*
Green Tea (Hyson)	*10/- to 18/-*	*14/- to 20/-*
Green Dust	*6/- to 8/-*	*8/- to 12/-*
Green & Imperial	*14/- to 18/-*	*16/- to 24/-*
Bloom Green	*16/- to 20/-*	*16/- to 26/-*
Finest Hyson	*—*	*36/-*

Bohea, Congo (or Congou) and Pekoe were black teas, with Bohea the most common coarse sort, and Congo and Pekoe the better qualities. Hyson was green, while Imperial was a term applied to medium teas. There were also: Caper and Gunpowder, green teas with a small, tightly rolled leaf; Twankey green, (from which we acquired the name of the famous pantomime character, Widow Twankey); Souchong, a large-leafed black tea; Bing, another medium type of tea; and Singlo, the lowest quality of the green teas.

Most people seem to have bought the more common black and green teas, Bohea and Hyson. Entries in Twinings' sales ledgers for 1715 and 1716 include the following:

Mrs Bankes [of Kingston Hall] ½ pound bohea at 18/- a lb

Mr Edward Stanley 12 lb finest bohea tea at 18/-
[an unusually large amount]

Mr Stoughton in April 1715 1 lb Bohea tea & a canister

5th October 1715 ½ lb Bohea tea at 18/- a lb

2nd Feb 1716 1 lb Bohea tea at 18/- a lb

16 May 1716 ½ lb Bohea tea at 18/- a lb

27 May 1 lb fine bohea tea & canister

Most tea was sold loose from the chest and customers bought quarter, half and one pound quantities, which were wrapped in a screw of paper. A written order sent with a servant on 14 August 1809 to William Miller, a Glasgow tea trader, instructed, 'if your 7/6 Black Tea be good at present, you may desire him to paper a pound of it strongly up, and pout in the mouth of the Barley packing'. Mr Miller added to the slip of paper, '28 lb Barley £0. 7. 6. 1 lb Tea £0. 7. 6'. Then, in 1826, a merchant by the name of John Horniman decided to package his teas in foil-lined paper packets to offer the public a more hygienic tea in standard, carefully weighed amounts. But his revolutionary idea did not catch on until the later part of the nineteenth century and Horniman struggled to distribute his blends. Because they were making good profits by selling their own blended and unblended loose teas, other tea traders would not handle his products, so he was obliged to market his teas through chemists' and confectioners' shops.

While taxation remained high and tea was an expensive commodity, it was not surprising that unscrupulous traders found ways of stretching supplies. Additives were mixed in, as condemned in an Act passed by the government in 1725: 'very great quantities of sloe leaves, liquorish leaves, and the leaves of tea that have been before used, or the leaves of other trees, shrubs or plants in imitation of tea ... and do likewise mix, colour, stain and dye such leaves, and likewise tea with terra japonica, sugar, molasses, clay, logwood and other ingredients, and do sell and vend the same as true and real tea, to the prejudice of the health of His Majesty's subjects, the diminution of the revenue and to the ruin of the fair trader'. Jonas Hanway, writing in 1756, confirmed the trade in used leaves: 'You have also heard, that your maids sometimes dry your leaves and sell them: the industrious nymph who is bent on gain may get a shilling a pound for such tea. These leaves are dyed in a solution of Japan earth ... .'

In 1785, Richard Twining explained the methods used in *Observations on the Tea & Window Act and on the Tea Trade*:

I shall here communicate to the Public a particular account of this manufacture, which I have lately received from a gentleman, who has made very accurate enquiries on the subject.

METHOD OF MAKING SMOUCH WITH ASH TREE LEAVES TO MIX WITH BLACK TEAS

When gathered they are first dried in the sun and then baked. They are next put on the floor and trod upon until the leaves are small, then lifted and steeped in copperas, with sheep's dung, after which, being dried on a floor, they are fit for use.

Twining suggested that in one small area of eight or nine miles, approximately 20 tons of 'smouch' was manufactured every year.

But the adulteration of tea leaves was not taking place just in England. It was also a Chinese practice to mix other substances with the tea. European and American consumers expected their expensive green teas to have a blue tinge to their colouring and so, as the great plant hunter, Robert Fortune, explained in 1852 in *A Journey to the Tea Countries of China*, the Chinese method had for some time been to 'crush Prussian Blue to a fine powder and add gypsum in a ration of three to four resulting in a light blue dye powder. Add the powder five minutes before the end of the last roasting'. A London newspaper, the *Family Herald*, commenting on Fortune's publication, said, 'We Englishmen swallow tea, go to bed, turn and toss, keep awake, get up, complain of unstrung nerves and weak digestion, and visit the doctor, who shakes his head and says, "tea!". This is what he says, but what he means is "Metallic paint".'

Because the consuming public knew that it was easier to adulterate green tea, more and more people began to buy only black. This may have marked the beginning of the British preference for black tea and a gradual decline in the amount of green purchased.

TEA AND POLITICS

People often wonder why it was that Great Britain became a tea-drinking nation while most of the rest of Europe took to coffee. There are probably two principal reasons. First, and perhaps more important, was the effect of the trade monopoly held by the English East India Company. Chartered by Elizabeth I in 1600, it was later granted remarkable powers by Charles II. As William Ukers explained in *All About Tea*,

It constituted not only the World's greatest tea monopoly but also the source of inspiration for the first English propaganda in behalf of a beverage. It was so powerful that it precipitated a dietetic revolution in England, changing the British people from a nation of potential coffee drinkers to a nation of tea drinkers, and all within the space of a few years. It was a formidable rival of states and empires, with power to acquire territory, coin money, command fortresses and troops, form alliances, make war and peace, and exercise both civil and criminal jurisdiction.

Secondly, at the end of the seventeenth century, England and Holland, at war with France, were practically forced out of the Mediterranean, making it difficult to acquire stocks of coffee from the Levant. This problem may well have recurred during the War of the Spanish Succession (1702–13) when England and Holland were together fighting Spain and France. With a steady supply of tea being shipped into London by the East India Company, the Chinese leaf provided a reliable alternative and became the preferred beverage.

Tea drinking developed along similar lines in North America. Emigrants from Britain, Holland and Portugal took their customs and equipage with them when they set sail across the Atlantic. When the English captured New Amsterdam from the Dutch and renamed it New York in 1674, tea was already well established as an everyday beverage for the wealthier members of the new society. The city opened its own pleasure gardens and coffee houses very like those in England, and with similar names. In 1682, William Penn founded the Quaker city of Philadelphia, advocating tea as the preferred drink because it filled 'the cups that cheer but not inebriate'. By the 1690s, apothecaries in Boston were advertising 'Green and Ordinary teas'. Whenever they went out to tea, ladies carried little bags that held a small teacup and saucer of the best china, and a spoon.

As in England, tea was not just for ladies. In December 1757 George Washington ordered from England six teapots and 12lb of tea, including Hyson and best green. His breakfast normally consisted of two cups of tea and three or four cakes of Indian corn meal, called how-cakes, which he ate with honey and butter. Inventories from the Washington household list all the equipage necessary for the serving of tea: caddies, boards, tables, cups and saucers, teaspoons, a copper kettle and a silver-plated urn.

The Cust Family of Belton by Enoch Seeman, c.1741–5. The widowed Anne Cust is shown seated at the tea table, surrounded by her children. One of her daughters takes charge of pouring the tea, a bowl of sugar with silver nippers sits ready to be offered with each cup. As in most paintings of early tea drinking, there is no evidence of milk.

The Boston Tea Party 1773, a hand-coloured print showing the 'Boston Boys' in native American dress, throwing chests of tea into the Charles River. It took three hours to hurl 340 chests overboard, and as they worked, the 'Mohawks' sang:

'Our Warrens here, and brave Revere, with hands to do and words to cheer for liberty and laws;

our countries 'braves' and true defenders shall ne'er be left by the North Enders fighting freedom's cause! then rally, boys, and hasten on to meet our chiefs at the Green Dragon!'

[James Warren and Paul Revere were prominent members of the opposition to British taxes]

But the history of tea drinking in the American colonies was not set to follow such a smooth path as in Britain. In 1767, Charles Townshend, the Chancellor of the Exchequer, pushed an Act through Parliament that allowed the government to raise revenue by taxing tea and other goods being purchased and imported to America for the purpose of maintaining the army and government officials there. The only way for the Americans to buy tea was through the English East India Company, approximately 90 per cent of it through the ports of Boston, New York and Philadelphia. Just as in Britain, there had always been a certain amount of contraband trade, especially via Holland.

Not only was the 1767 Act extremely unpopular in America, but Parliament then added insult to injury by introducing much stricter law enforcement against smuggling. Most American ports reacted by refusing to allow dutiable goods to be landed, while smugglers campaigned by linking their illegal activities with a struggle for freedom from an oppressive government. Parliament gave way, repealing the Townshend Act, and peace was restored. In 1773, however, a new Act was passed that gave the East India Company the right to ship tea direct to America and sell it through its agents without paying any duties. This monopoly outraged the colonial tea merchants and shippers who quickly realised that they would be ruined. So, when the Company sent 600,000 tons of tea on seven ships, hostilities bubbled to the surface once again and erupted in demonstrations. In New York and Philadelphia, the ships were forced back. In Charleston, customs officers seized the tea. In Boston, it provoked the famous Tea Party.

When the *Dartmouth* sailed into Boston harbour, she was allowed to unload all her cargo except the tea. Having completed all the usual paperwork, she could not legally set sail again for England with the tea still on board so she was forced to remain in the harbour. At a town meeting on 29 November 1773, a suggestion to destroy the tea was rejected. However, the seething anti-British feelings amongst the local people, including some highly respected members of society, brought things to a head on 16 December. During a final meeting to try to solve the problem, a group of local men, disguised as native Americans (as a symbol of the oppressed people of the colony) barged into the hall shouting, 'Boston harbour a teapot tonight.' A band of 20 or 30 men, disguised in the same native Indian outfits, boarded the *Dartmouth* and hurled the chests of tea overboard.

The young ladies of Boston signed a pledge, 'We the daughters of those patriots who have, and do now appear for the public interest, and in that principally regard their posterity, as such do with pleasure engage with them in denying ourselves the drinking of foreign tea, in hopes to frustrate a plan that tends to deprive a whole community of all that is valuable to life.' They were joined by others around the country, drinking instead 'Balsamic hyperion' made from dried raspberry leaves, or infusions of other herbs.

The Boston Tea Party did not destroy the American taste for tea, although few retailers in Boston dared to offer it for sale for a number of years. George and Martha Washington continued to serve the best quality tea and in 1796, the artist Benjamin Henry Latrobe sketched the President taking tea on the porch at Mount Vernon. Others followed suit, drinking tea in the same way as the British, as an after-dinner drink. In 1827 a servant in Boston published a book of instructions on how to conduct formal tea-parties. Tea was poured into cups, which were then handed round on trays with jugs of cream, bowls of sugar, and plates of toast, bread and butter, and cakes. When guests had finished their tea, the cups were collected and washed, before refills were offered.

TEA FOR THE LOWER CLASSES

The vast amount of duty-free, smuggled tea coming into Britain not only went to the rich, it also helped the poor to obtain their weekly ration. However, it was still not cheap. As we have seen, an unskilled man earned only 10 shillings a week, while a skilled worker could expect between 15 shillings and a guinea (£1 1s 0d). And many felt that tea was not an appropriate drink for the working classes. Writing in Scotland in 1744, Duncan Forbes' outrage is only too apparent: 'But when the opening of a Trade with the East India brought the Price of Tea so low that the meanest labouring Man could compass the Purchase of it … . When Sugar, the inseparable Companion of Tea, came to be in the Possession of the very poorest Housewife, where formerly it had been a great Rarity – and thereby was at hand to mix with water and Brandy, or Rum – and when Tea and Punch became thus the Diet and Debauch of all the beer and Ale Drinkers, the Effects were suddenly and very severely felt.'

This view was supported by Jonas Hanway in *A Journal of Eight Days' Journey*: 'The use of tea descended to the Plebœan order among us, about the beginning of the century… . Men seem to have lost their stature, and comeliness, and women their beauty. Your very chambermaids have lost their bloom, I suppose by sipping tea … . It is the curse of this nation, that the laborer and mechanic will ape the lord … .'

Household servants, having developed a liking for the beverage favoured by their employers, often had their wages calculated to include a tea allowance. At Saltram House in Devon in the 1780s, ledgers of wages paid include 'Feb 19th To Jane Dowie – for nine months wages – fifteen pounds, fifteen shillings. Her allowance of tea – one pound, six shillings'. And an Italian visitor to England in 1755 noted that 'even the common maid servants must have their tea twice a day in all parade of quality; they make it their bargain at first; this very article amounts to as much as the wages of servants in Italy'.

Fair-minded employers provided tea free as a daily perk – perhaps the fore-runner of the workplace 'tea break'. Dr Aiken of Manchester wrote in 1790 that 'somewhat before 1760, a considerable manufacturer allocated a back parlour with a fire for the use of his apprentices, and gave them tea twice a day'. At the complex that made up Quarry Bank in Cheshire, £9 3s was spent on tea for the workers in the cotton mill in September 1794. At the Apprentice House, where pauper children from Liverpool and Manchester were accommodated, 4 shillings was spent on tea and 7 shillings on sugar in 1814. And one of the millworkers at Quarry Bank, Joseph Sefton, in an account of the diet presented to magistrates, stated: 'On Sunday we had for dinner boiled pork and potatoes. We also had peas, beans, turnips and cabbages in their season. Monday, we had for dinner milk and bread and sometimes thick porridge … .' Each day, he said, was much the same, 'We had only water to drink, when ill, we were allowed tea.'

Others were not so generous or tolerant, as highlighted in a letter to the editor of the *Lady's Monthly Museum or Polite Repository* in 1801: 'During a late excursion to Brighton … . I found nothing but young ladies … all anxious for places, and wished to go out to service … one of them informed me that she had lately left her place and could have an excellent character [reference], her only reason for quitting being that her mistress did not suffer her to drink tea twice a day, and could not abide her wearing feathers in her hat on Sunday … .'

The habits of servants were highlighted in *A Poem Upon Tea* by Duncan Campbell.

L = Lady of the House
V = Visitor

V: (drinking tea poured by Lady of the House):
I have some TEA, I thought was good before;
Now I'm resolv'd to give it to the Poor:
My Suky Dainty and Bess Taste, the Cook,
Will drink it sitting in the Chimney-nook,
I often catch them draining what I leave:

L: Poor honest Girls, they love it, I perceive.

The doll's house at Nostell Priory in Yorkshire, which was made for the Winn family c.1735. According to family tradition it was the work of the young Thomas Chippendale, although there is no firm evidence to support this. Almost all the original furnishings survive, providing a valuable picture of an eighteenth-century house, above and below stairs. A silver kettle is shown on a stand in the kitchen, while a silver tea set is laid out in the Red Drawing Room on the floor above.

THE DISTREST POET.

The social commentator, Arthur Young, was, like so many others at the time, somewhat shocked in 1767 by 'labourers losing their time to come and go to the tea table; nay farmers' servants even demanding tea for their breakfast with the maids'. But it was not quite as simple as that. In his 1795 publication, *The Case of the Labourers in Husbandry*, David Davies, Rector of Barkham in Berkshire, wrote, 'Why should such people, it is asked, indulge in a luxury which is only proper for their betters; and not rather content themselves with milk, which is in every form wholesome and nourishing? Were it true that poor people could everywhere procure so excellent an article as milk, there would be then just reason to reproach them for giving preference to the miserable infusion of which they are so fond. But it is not so. Wherever the poor can get milk, do they not gladly use it? And where they cannot get it, would they not gladly exchange their tea for it?'

What the haughty and critical forgot was that land enclosure had, in one fell swoop, removed the possibility for hundreds of thousands of people to keep their own cow and had therefore also deprived them of a regular supply of milk, butter and cheese. The low wages earned from labouring did not allow families to buy relatively expensive dairy products, while a little tea could be stretched to brew a hot, filling, comforting drink when food was short. As Davies explained to his readers, 'Still you exclaim, Tea is a luxury. If you mean fine hyson tea, sweetened with refined sugar, and softened with cream, I readily admit it to be so. But this is not the tea of the poor. Spring water, just coloured with a few leaves of the lowest-priced tea, and sweetened with the brownest sugar [a good deal cheaper than refined sugar], is the luxury for which you reproach them. To this they have recourse for mere necessity: and were they now to be deprived of this, they would immediately be reduced to bread and water. Tea-drinking is not the cause but the consequence of the distress of the poor.'

But it is the words of Isaac D'Israeli, father of the future Prime Minister, that best sum up the widespread acceptance of tea throughout Britain at the end of the Georgian era:

The progress of this famous plant has been something like the progress of truth; suspected at first, though very palatable to those who had the courage to taste it; resisted as it encroached; abused as its popularity seemed to spread; and establishing its triumph at last, in cheering the whole land from the palace to the cottage, only by the slow and resistless efforts of time and its own virtues.

The Distressed Poet, *engraved by William Hogarth in 1740. Despite the dire poverty and lack of furniture, the teapot stands firmly on the overmantel of the fireplace as one of the necessities for life.*

HOW AND WHEN TEA WAS DRUNK

ETIQUETTE AND RITUALS

As tea was a relatively new commodity, and despite the fact that more and more people were brewing and drinking it, not everyone knew exactly what to do with the leaves. The poet Robert Southey recounted a story in his *Commonplace Book* of 1850 about 'the first pound of tea that ever came to Penrith [in Cumberland]. It was sent as a present without directions how to use it. They boiled the whole at once in a kettle, and sat down to eat the leaves with butter and salt; and they wondered how anybody could like such a dish.'

The tradition of the lady of the house brewing and pouring the tea herself continued. Sugar was almost universally taken – refined white sugar for the rich and dark brown unrefined sugar, molasses or treacle for the poor. In 1706, a certain Dr Duncan explained that 'Coffee, Chocolate and Tea were at first us'd only as Medicines while they continued unpleasant, but since they were made delicious with sugar, they are become poison.' François de La Rochefoucauld, writer and traveller, wrote in 1784 in *A Frenchman in England*: 'The high cost of sugar or molasses, of which large quantities are required, does not prevent this custom being a universal one, to which there are no exceptions.'

Right: Anti-Saccharrites *by James Gillray, published in 1792. George III, his Queen and their daughters are shown boycotting sugar as part of the anti-slave movement. Since most English tea drinkers had always added sugar to their tea, the taste of the beverage without the sweetener did not please 'John Bull's family', as can be seen in their faces.*

Left: A Meissen sugar basin, c.1725, decorated with Chinese figures.

Milk or cream was added by most people who could afford it. Per Kalm in his *Account of His Visit to England on his Way to America* in 1748 observed that 'most people pour a little cream or sweet milk into the teacup when they are about to drink the tea'. And although in 1782, the traveller John Byng, Lord Torrington, noted in his diary that he drank tea at an inn in Bagshot in Surrey 'with the novelty of cream', the practice seems to have been well established long before. The Viscount obviously found that he much preferred cream to milk and described how he breakfasted one morning with 'an indulgence of appetite ... by swallowing 3 hot rolls and a pint of cream with my tea'.

In 1729, in *The Journal of a Modern Lady*, Jonathan Swift described a typical morning in the eponymous lady's house:

Now, loit'ring o'er her tea and cream,
She enters on her usual theme;
Her last night's ill success repeats
Call Lady Spade a hundred cheats

And Samuel Johnson, famous for his love of tea, summed up his own preference:

So hear it then, my Rennie dear,
Nor hear it with a frown;
You cannot make the tea so fast
As I can gulp it down.
I therefore pray thee, Rennie dear,
That thou wilt give to me
With cream and sugar softened well,
Another dish of tea.

Edward Young's poem, 'The Love of Fame, the Universal passion', *c.*1725, indicates how tea bowls were held in the eighteenth century and how elegant tea drinkers could look while lifting the exquisite porcelain to their lips.

Her two red lips affected Zephyrs blow,
To cool the Bohea, and inflame the Beau;
While one white Finger and a Thumb conspire
To lift the Cup and make the World admire.

William Hogarth's portrait of The Wollaston Family, *painted in 1730, shortly after William Wollaston inherited the family estates. The painting is thronged with relatives, including several wealthy merchants and City figures. William is shown flanked by card and tea tables. The lady on the far right is handing back her cup, turned upside down on its saucer, to indicate that she has drunk enough.*

TEA AT BREAKFAST

At the beginning of the eighteenth century, tea was still not widely drunk at breakfast, with alcohol still prevailing in many homes. But Mackintosh of Borkim in Scotland noted in 1729, 'When I came to my friend's house of a morning, I used to be asked if I had my morning draught yet? I am now asked if I have had my tea? And in lieu of the big quaigh [a large drinking vessel] with strong ale and toast, and after a dram of good wholesome Scots spirits, there is now the tea-kettle put to the fire, the tea table and silver and china equippage brought in and marmalade and cream.'

As the century progressed, in all but the poorest households, the day began with a breakfast of tea served with bread and toast and butter. Per Kalm observed in 1748,

Breakfast, which here in England was almost everywhere partaken by those more comfortably off, consisted in drinking Tea, but not as we do in Sweden, when we take a quantity of hot water on an empty stomach, without anything else to it, but the English fashion was somewhat more natural, for they ate at the same time one or more slices of wheat-bread, which they had first toasted at the fire, and when it was very hot, had spread butter on it, and then placed it a little way from the fire on the hearth, so that the butter might melt well into the bread.

François de La Rochefoucauld described a typical English breakfast in an upper-class home in 1784: 'The commonest breakfast is at 9 o'clock and by that time the ladies are fully dressed with their hair properly done for the day. Breakfast consists of tea and bread and butter in various forms. In the houses of the rich, you have coffee, chocolate and so on. The morning newspapers are on the table and those who want to do so, read them during breakfast.' In the

The morning room at Saltram. If the Parker family were entertaining, breakfast would be taken here from 10.30am, with an urn and cistern of black tea at one end of the table, and another of green tea at the other.

early nineteenth century, the Rev. Thomas Talbot, while staying with his sister, Frances Parker, at Saltram House, wrote letters to his wife telling her of life in the house – often in rather barbed tones. If there were no house guests, breakfast 'of the plainest description', was taken in the Blue Bow Room on the first floor. When guests were staying, breakfast was eaten in the morning room at 10.30, 'or whenever eight or so of the party have appeared…. An urn and cistern of black tea at one end – ditto of green tea at the other and coffee at the side – the breakfasts and bread by no means good.'

Breakfast parties were given by the fashionable, sometimes in the bedroom, at other times in the breakfast room. On 9 August 1768, the Rev. Woodforde recorded in his diary, 'Mrs Melliar gives a public breakfast at the Cary Vicarage in honour of Lord Stavordale's coming of age…. There was dancing in the garden till three in the afternoon.'

For the poor, the first meal of the day during the early part of the century was accompanied by ale or beer, but tea gradually replaced alcohol. Although it was still more expensive than many of the labouring classes could easily afford, a paper entitled *The Good and Bad Effects of Tea*, written in 1758, confirms the habit:

Tea is taken in a Morning as a Meal; the Method of making it is so well known as to require no Directions; some like cream and sugar in it, other only one, and some drink it without either cream or sugar, and these, I think the most polite. A very material Part of the Breakfast is a good Toast and Butter, or, as they like, Bread spread with Butter, or a hot Roll, well buttered; the Tea serves to wash down the more substantial part of the Breakfast, and without these necessary concomitants, such as have good appetites, will be disappointed from Tea only.

Per Kalm noted that, 'The servants in London also commonly get such a breakfast [ie tea with bread and butter] but in the country they have to content themselves with whatever else they can get.' Working people could buy tea for breakfast on their way to their offices and shops. An advertisement in a London newspaper announced: 'This is to give notice, to all Ladies and Gentlemen, at Spencer's Original Breakfasting Hut, between Sir Hugh Middleton's Head and Saint John-street Road by the New River Side, fronting Saddler's Wells, may be had every morning, except Sundays, fine tea, sugar, bread, butter, and milk, at 4d. per head: coffee at 3d. a dish. And in the afternoon, tea, sugar, and milk, at 3d. per head, with good attendance.'

Silver urn by Thomas Heming, 1769, in the morning room at Saltram. The urn became more and more popular from the 1770s, the most fashionable shape resembling a vase on a stemmed foot. The water was kept hot by a red-hot cylindrical box-iron in a cavity in the body of the urn, or by burning charcoal in the base.

TEA AFTER DINNER

The time of dinner began the century at any hour between 2 and 4pm, but gradually moved later, into the late afternoon and early evening. When the last of the food had been eaten, the men remained sitting at the dining table with their pipes of tobacco and bottles of wine, claret and port. There they might indulge in two or more hours of conversation and drinking. The women moved to a withdrawing room to chat and drink tea, where they might be joined later by the men. According to La Rochefoucauld, 'At the end of two or three hours, a servant announces that tea is ready and conducts the gentlemen from their drinking to join the ladies in the drawing-room, where they are usually employed making tea and coffee. After making tea, one generally plays whist, and at midnight there is cold meat for those who are hungry.'

In some cases houses were redesigned to provide a suitable area for tea drinking. In 1752, George Lyttelton, later Lord Lyttelton of Hagley Hall in Worcester-shire, wrote to his architect to say that 'Lady Lyttelton wishes for a room of separation between the eating room and the drawing room, to hinder the ladies from the noise and talk of the men when left to their bottle, which must sometime happen, even at Hagley'. Dunham Massey in Cheshire had a room, still called the Tea Room, which was only used for the service of tea (and coffee and chocolate) after dinner. At Claydon House in Buckinghamshire a very exotic tea room was installed by the Verneys in the 1760s. The Chinese Room was an intimate sitting room on the upper floor where the family would take tea sitting on a divan in an alcove, surrounded by exuberant plasterwork in the form of a Chinese fretwork tea house.

Far left: Detail from the richly decorated plasterwork in the Chinese Room at Claydon House, modelled by Luke Lightfoot in the 1760s. Lightfoot created his version of an oriental tea ceremony to decorate the frieze, as the Verney family would have taken tea here, sitting on a divan. This practice clearly continued into the twentieth century, as shown in this photograph (left).

A very early example of just such an evening at the court of William and Mary at Kensington Palace, dating from the late seventeenth century, was recalled by Lionel, Lord Buckhurst, later 1st Duke of Dorset:

King William, like almost all Dutchmen, never failed to attend the tea-table every evening. It happened that her Majesty [Queen Mary] having one afternoon by his desire made tea, and waiting for the King's arrival, who was engaged on business in his cabinet at the other extreme of the gallery, the boy [aged four] hearing the Queen express her impatience at the delay, ran away to the closet, dragging after him his cart. When he arrived at the door, he knocked, and the king asking 'Who is there?' 'Lord Buck', answered he. 'And what does Lord Buck want with me?' replied his Majesty. 'You must come to tea directly,' said he, 'the Queen is waiting for you.'

However, unlike the king, not all men enjoyed this rather feminine activity. John Byng wrote in his diary in 1794 that he went riding after dinner one day but was driven back by rain. 'At my return I found Mrs B at tea, with some ladies of our house; and joining them, pass'd a dull hour in the much no-discourse of a tea table....' And Jonathan Swift in *The Journey of a Modern Lady*, 1729, found that female tea drinkings could be most unattractive occasions with hostesses often:

*Surrounded with the noisy clans
Of prudes, coquettes and harridans*

Tea was also used as a flavouring. This very early example comes from a book of 'Receits' kept by Mary Booth, daughter of the 2nd Earl of Warrington, at Dunham Massey in Cheshire. The book probably dates from the 1730s:

Take a pint and half of cream, eight eggs leaving out the whites: beat your eggs very well and put about half your cream to them, and as much sugar as you think will sweeten it. Then take the other half of your cream with about half an ounce of your finest green tea, and stew them together until you think you have got all the flavour and colour of the tea. Then strain through a lawn sieve in the other half of your cream and eggs; stir it over a slow fire until it grows thick: keep it stirring 'till it is almost cold, then pour it into your dish and serve it up. If you have any Naples Biscuits, you may ornament it at top in flowers or as you please. You may if you like it, colour with Pastatichio Nuts or spinage juice, but it is reckon'd better without.

The tea-table makes a frequent appearance in Georgian caricatures, probably because it formed such an important part of the social scene. In Miseries Personal, *published in 1807, Thomas Rowlandson, evokes the despair of a hostess providing tea and coffee for 'half a score of ... formal females' in the drawing room, while their gentlemen drink port and discuss politics at the dining table.*

Pub June 2 1807 by R. Ackermann N 101 Strand

MISERIES PERSONAL.

After Dinner when the ladies retire with you from a party of very pleasant men, having to entertain as you can, half a score of, empty, or formal females then after a decent time has elap-
-ed your patience and topics are equally exhausted ringing for the Tea &c. which you sit making in despair, for above two hours, having three or four times sent word to the gentlemen that it is
ready, and overheard your husband at the last message answer "Very well — another bottle of wine" — By the time that the tea and coffee are quite cold, they arrive, continuing as they enter and for an hour
afterwards their political disputes, occasionally suspended by the master of the house by a reasonable complaint to his lady, at the coldness of the coffee — soon after the carriages are announced & the company disperse

Rowlandson inv. 1807

TEA FOR VISITORS

In the sixteenth and seventeenth centuries, visitors to private houses were usually offered sweetmeats or different kinds of cakes, fruits of the season, and some sort of alcoholic beverage. This tradition continued into the eighteenth century, but tea was just beginning to make an impact as an afternoon drink, even though it had yet to take on the role of a formal meal. Dr Aiken describes this transition in his 1795 publication, *The History of Manchester*:

About 1720, there were not above three or four carriages kept in the town. One of those belonged to Madame — in Salford. This respectable old lady was of a social disposition, and could not bring herself to conform to the new-fashioned beverage of tea and coffee; whenever, therefore, she made her afternoon visits, her friends presented her with a tankard of ale and a pipe of tobacco. A little before this period a country gentleman had married the daughter of a citizen of London; she had been used to tea, and in compliment to her it was introduced by some of her neighbours.

Another doctor, Alex Carlyle, writing in his autobiography set in Harrogate in Yorkshire in 1763, noted 'The ladies gave afternoon's tea and coffee in their turn, which coming but once in four or six weeks amounted to a trifle.' This may be proof that regular tea-parties were rather an expensive way of entertaining, but this is contradicted by the account of Miss Thackeray, a daughter of a Cambridge surgeon, who pronounced tea-time 'an inexpensive mode of seeing company. A cow which we kept in a field supplied us with plenty of cream for the tea, and we always had a common cake to cut. Thus was frugality and hospitality combined, the family was too large (there were thirteen children) for ostentatious luxuries.'

Tea thus became more and more the fashionable refreshment that was offered to visitors to the house. Countless entries in diaries for the eighteenth and nineteenth centuries record the serving of tea during visits to and from friends and neighbours. Thomas Turner of West Hoathly in Sussex was obviously an avid tea drinker: his diaries show that four or five times each week he drank tea at one or other of his neighbours' houses. The following entries are typical:

*1755 Sunday 7th September
After church, Master Piper stayed and smoked a pipe with me. After we drank tea, my wife and I took a walk.*

*1756 Wednesday 21st January
Halland gardener cut my grape-vine and drank tea with us.*

*1756 Monday 16th August
We came away about 3 o'clock, and called at my Aunt Ovendean's, drank tea and came home about 8.35.*

*1759 Tuesday 23rd October
My wife and I had an invitation to Halland to drink tea and sup there with a great many more, there being a rejoicing on account of the taking of Quebec*

The diaries of John Salusbury of Leighton Buzzard in Bedfordshire are full of similar references. Salusbury was a bachelor, whose chief amusements were card playing, dancing, shooting, smoking, fishing and tea drinking and he recorded how, almost every day, he took tea with friends or neighbours:

1755 August 14th
After evening service drank tea and spent the evening at Mr Ward's, and smoaked a pipe with Capt. Hutton in the summer house.

1755 October 6th
Drank tea & spent the evening at Mr Ward's with Mrs Hutton.

1757 November 6th
After dinner, Mr Snablin & I walked to Heath and drank tea with Capt. And Madam and one Mr Sherrard, a Barbadoes surgeon who is on a visit here.

1755 May 14th
Mr & Mrs Ward came after evening prayers, drank tea and supped with me

1758 October 4th
Dined at Mr Capon's but came away after tea.

Even upper-class boys, away at public school, were now drinking tea. William Dutton wrote to his father from Eton in 1766, 'I wish you would be so kind as to let me have Tea and Sugar here to drink in the afternoon, without which there is no such thing as keeping company with boys of standing.' And Richard How wrote from Wandsworth, south-west of London, to his mother in Gracechurch Street in the City in 1739, 'Honoured Mother, I receiv'd my uncle Kingsberg's Letter; and the shirt, which was sent me last Night, fits me very well, only it is rather too strait in the Neck. I should be glad if thou wou'dst please send me some Tea; for that which I had has been gone a long while.' Jonathan Swift poked fun at students who neglected their studies because of tea: 'the fear of being thought pedants hath taken many young divines off from their severer studies, which they have exchanged for plays, in order to qualify them for the tea table.'

A poem published anonymously in Dublin in 1725 describes a grand lady calling at various houses to take tea with sugar and cream:

The leading Fair the Word harmonious gives
Betty around attends with bended knee.
Each white arm Fair, the painted cup receives;
Pours the rich Cream, or stirs the sweetened Tea.

TEA FOR PARTIES

Tea was also now the favourite refreshment at larger gatherings and parties. Frances Bankes wrote from her home at Kingston Hall to her mother to describe such an event, which she called a 'fete', held on 23 December 1791:

My bedroom had a long Table rather narrow made exactly to fit from the foot of the bed to the bottom of the room in the way of a Bar at an Inn, which was covered with Table cloths that reached the ground upon which there was Tea, white and red wine Negus, Orgeat [a syrup or cooling drink made originally from barley, subsequently from almonds, and orange-flavoured water], Lemonade and everything that people usually call for upon these occasions. The long Table above mentioned had a very good effect, Mr Bankes's Dressing Room and the side of my Bedroom where the Fireplace is, was occupied by the Tea- makers, who by that means could go in and out for everything they wanted without disturbing the Company. Upon Mr Bankes's Dressing Room Fire, we kept a Quantity of water constantly boiling, so that I flatter myself there never was so large a Company better supplied with hot Tea and Negus…. We had ten Ladies' Maids including Nancy and Gagnon who waited at the Tea table, and they all happened by accident to be dressed exactly alike – in pink and white, which had a very good effect.

Mrs Bankes's five children, allowed to stay up for the fun, were having such a wonderful time that 'when I came to Anne to propose at twelve o'clock that she should go to bed, she appeared in violent spirits and begged she might sit up as long as the other Ladies, but I took her and George with me into the Tea Room, gave them a great deal of bread and milk and water and put them to Bed'.

Masquerades, musical entertainments and ridottos (combining dancing with a concert) became popular both at home and in public assembly rooms. Such events usually included card playing, tea drinking and supper, with each activity taking place in different rooms. At Leinster House in Ireland, home of the Duke and Duchess of Leinster, 'We dine at half past four or five – go to tea, so to cards about nine – play till supper time – 'tis pretty late by the time we go to bed.'

An engraving of The Country Dance *by William Hogarth, 1735, showing a very mixed assembly summoning up a thirst before taking tea.*

TEA HOUSES

If at home, family and guests might wander into the garden to take tea, possibly in a temple or folly. This represents a progression from the custom of serving the third course or banquet of a grand Tudor or Stuart dinner in a banqueting house on the roof or in the grounds of the main house. Thus, for instance, Bess of Hardwick had a banqueting house on the leads of the roof at Hardwick Hall, where she would serve her guests sweetmeats, fruit and sweet wines. Indeed, former banqueting houses often became tea houses in the eighteenth century. At Mount Stewart in County Down, Northern Ireland, a Temple of the Winds, built as a banqueting house with vaulted basement and passageway running to a wine cellar and scullery, probably also provided shelter for after-dinner tea on warm summer afternoons and evenings.

The earliest recorded 'Tea House' or 'China House' was built in the 1640s at Beckett in Oxfordshire. It was a simple square building of one floor with a central door and two windows. At Cliveden in Buckinghamshire, the Venetian architect, Giacomo Leoni, designed c.1735 an Octagon Temple for Lord Orkney. Perched on the edge of a cliff overlooking the Thames, it provided spectacular views from the Prospect Room in the upper

storey, while below, there was 'a little cool room by way of grotto'. This temple for tea still stands, though it was converted into a chapel in the late nineteenth century.

At Weston Hall, Capability Brown laid out the gardens in the 1770s for Sir Henry Bridgeman. A Temple of Diana was designed by James Paine to stand beside the Temple Pool. It contained a circular tea room, an octagonal music room, an orangery and a bedroom for the dairywoman, who no doubt prepared the tea when required.

The Castle in the gardens at Saltram. This was built in the Gothick style by Theresa Parker in the early 1770s as a room where visitors might pause during their perambulations, to take tea and enjoy views out to the park.

Landscape gardens provided wonderful opportunities for buildings in which to take tea. The garden at Stourhead in Wiltshire included a rustic cottage, a Temple of the Sun, a Temple of Flora, a Pantheon and a Turkish Tent: outings would almost certainly have been made to one or other of these for tea. At Stowe in Buckinghamshire, after-dinner customs of the main house were reflected in the landscape garden in the 1740s. Lord Cobham and his Whig allies, the Pitts, Grenvilles and Lytteltons – known as the 'Boy Patriots' – would retire to the Temple of Friendship where they would drink port and discuss politics. Lady Cobham, meanwhile, would withdraw to the Ladies' Temple (later renamed the Queen's Temple) with her friends to take tea and to carry out the needlework and shellwork that once adorned the walls.

A tea house still stands in the grounds of Charles James Fox's house at St Anne's Hill in Wandsworth. The two-storey building has gothic arches at the entrance and set into the opposite wall, the decorations on walls and ceiling are of imitation stalactites and shells, the floor is of pebbles laid out in geometric designs, and a wooden staircase leads up to the balcony where Fox is said to have taken tea.

If there was no suitable building, a marquee was erected in the garden for

summer entertaining. A collection of letters written by the Williamson family in Bedfordshire between 1748 and 1765 includes one sent from Southampton in 1762. It reads 'Before breakfast we ranged the garden o'er picking the choicest fruits and flowers; from breakfast to dinner we read; after dinner drank your health every day in claret or madeira, sauntered about till tea, which we drank under a tent pitched in a close adjoining the gardens, where we could see the ships pass about 9 miles off; after that every even our horses were brought to the tent door, when we mounted and took a ride of 12 or 14 miles … which brought 9 o'clock and supper.'

An eighteenth-century painting of Cliveden, showing the Octagon Temple where Lord Orkney and his guests could drink tea overlooking the River Thames.

TEA IN THE COFFEE HOUSES AND PLEASURE GARDENS

The popularity of coffee houses continued throughout the eighteenth century. Here men could conduct their business, socialise, discuss politics and enjoy all-male company, while their ladies drank their tea at home with their family and friends. In 1714, Daniel Defoe was enjoying the busy social life of London: 'I am lodged in the street called Pall Mall, the ordinary residence of all strangers, because of its vicinity to the Queen's Palace, the Park, the Parliament House, the theatres and the chocolate and coffee houses where the best company frequent. If you would know our manner of living, 'tis thus: We rise by Nine, and those that frequent men's levees find entertainment at them till eleven, or, as in Holland go to the tea tables. About twelve the beau monde assemble in several coffee or chocolate houses ....'

For the working classes, what social life they had centred around the inns, taverns and ale houses, but an alternative attraction by this time – at least for those living in and around London – was provided by the pleasure gardens. Many of these, such as Sadlers Wells and New Tunbridge Wells in Clerkenwell, just north-west of the City, had started life as medicinal watering places. Others

developed around inns and taverns. Gardens were created and refreshment rooms, dance halls, gaming tables, skittle alleys and raffling shops added. Entertainments included walks through colourful gardens, horse riding, firework displays, circus acts, boat rides and tea drinking. Many were frequented by rough and bawdy groups of people – prostitutes, gamblers, drunks, rowdy young apprentices, and petty criminals – causing them to be closed down by the 1790s. Others were more genteel, attracting men, women and children from all classes, including the wealthy, the fashionable and even the royal family.

The Prussian Duc d'Archenholz observed at the end of the century: 'The English take a great delight in the public gardens, near the metropolis, where they assemble and drink tea together in the open air. The number of these in the neighbourhood of the capital is amazing, and the order, regularity, neatness, and even elegance of them are truly admirable. They are, however, rarely frequented by people of fashion; but the middle and lower ranks go there often, and seem much delighted with the music of an organ which is usually played in an adjoining building.'

Francis Place, political reformer and social commentator, remembered that

when he was a child in the 1780s, 'It was my father's custom as it was that of a vast many others who were house-keepers, well-doing persons, and persons of business ... to go to some public garden on a Sunday afternoon to drink tea, smoke, and indulge themselves with liquor. My father's principal place to resort was Bagnigge Wells then standing in the fields.' Bagnigge, just off what is now King's Cross Road, was opened in 1759. Its extensive gardens were laid out with formal walks, clipped hedges, statues, a grotto, a temple, ponds with goldfish, a banqueting hall and little arbours covered with sweetbriar roses and honeysuckle where tea was served.

At some, the cost of refreshment was included in the entrance fee. At others, customers were charged according to what they chose. In 1744, an advertisement in the *Daily Advertiser* announced that at Mulberry Gardens' Coffee House in Clerkenwell, 'Gentlemen and Ladies will be accommodated with breakfasting in the morning, and Coffee and Tea in the afternoon, with bread and butter, at fourpence per head, and without threepence per head.'

White Conduit House in Islington also offered its customers a large garden with 'pleasing walks, prettily disposed', 'genteel boxes' painted in the Flemish

The assembly at Bagnigge Wells, in north-east London, from a drawing by J.Sanders and J.R.Smith published in 1772. The gardens of Bagnigge House, originally the country residence of Nell Gwynn, were opened to the public in 1758. In David Garrick's farce Bon Ton, 1775, a woman from the city says:

Bone Tone's the space 'twixt Saturday and Monday,
And riding in a one-horse chair on Sunday.
'tis drinking tea on summer afternoons
At Bagnigge Wells with China and gilt spoons

style and little arbours all around for tea drinking. Tea at White Conduit had its own code of behaviour when it came to flirtation and courtship. If a gentleman wished to make the acquaintance of a particular lady, it was the accepted practice to tread on her skirt, as if by accident, apologise profusely for such clumsy behaviour and then to offer an adjournment to an arbour for tea in order to make amends. By the end of the century, the garden often took more than £50 each Sunday afternoon from the sale of its sixpenny tickets that bought tea and slices of the famous bread made on the premises and as popular as traditional Chelsea buns. 'White Conduit loaves!' was one of the cries of London and was listened out for by ladies who purchased them to serve with tea to their guests.

Probably the best known of all London's pleasure gardens was Vauxhall, south of the river in Lambeth. Variously known as Fulke's Hall, Faukeshall and Foxhall, Vauxhall opened in 1732 and reached the height of its success in the second half of the century. As well as tea, there were promenades, a temple, a lily pond, firework displays, concerts, Indian jugglers, equestrian entertainments, balloon ascents, elaborate illuminations, and pavilions with supper boxes for six to eight people.

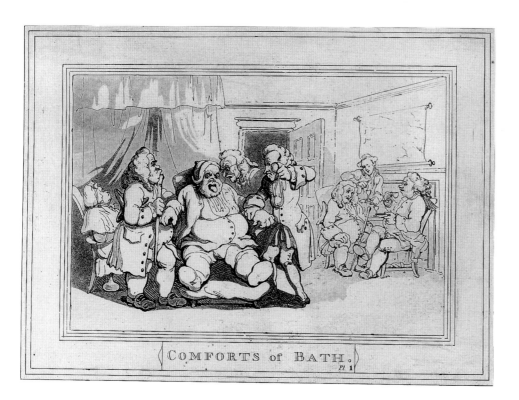

COMFORTS of BATH.
Pl. 1

Thomas Rowlandson's view of the Comforts of Bath, *published in 1798. The days spent relaxing and taking the spring waters were treated as a rest cure from the over-indulgence of everyday life. In* The Pickwick Papers *Charles Dickens described 'Bath being full, the company and the sixpences for tea, poured in, in shoals…. In the tea-room, and hovering round the card tables, were vast numbers of queer old ladies and decrepit old gentlemen, discussing all the small talk and scandal of the day….'*

TEA IN THE SPA TOWNS

Outside London, visitors flocked to the spa towns – old-established resorts such as Bath in Somerset and Tunbridge Wells in Kent, and more recently established spas such as Buxton in Derbyshire, created by the Duke of Devonshire, and the Yorkshire resorts of Harrogate and Scarborough. Here, too, tea played a vitally important part of each day's social life. Idle days could be spent taking the waters, attending the theatre, opera or horse races, promenading elegantly in parks and gardens, partaking in smart society events at assembly rooms, and, of course, taking tea in a genteel fashion and with perfect manners.

In 1757, Mrs Philip Lybbe Powys of Hardwicke House in Oxfordshire, wrote about her time in Buxton, 'Sir Harry Hemloak, his two sisters, and more company returned with us, and about ten we went to the Assembly Room, where the Duke of Devonshire always presided as master of ceremonies, and after the ball gave an elegant cold supper … we got home about five. The next evening were at the concert, as the same company usually met at that on the second night, and on the third day again went to the course. There came back with us to tea the Duke of Devonshire, Mr and Mrs Simpson, and two Miss Bourns.'

In Bath, the day began with early bathing in one of the five baths, then came a visit to the Pump Room to drink the mineral waters, to chat and listen to the band. Before breakfast, the company would proceed to a refreshment house for coffee and time to read the newspapers, write letters, and talk. Breakfast parties were then held in the public gardens or assembly houses and sometimes included concerts, lectures and dancing. After breakfast came church services and then, at noon, people would promenade around the town, to take the air and generally mingle. In the afternoon, dinner was eaten earlier than in London and was followed by evening prayers and a further visit to the Pump Room. More promenading was followed by tea at the assembly rooms, while the later part of the evening was spent at the theatre, dancing, gambling or visiting friends.

Bath's New Assembly Rooms were opened in 1771 and it is clear from the minutes of the committee meetings that took place prior to the official opening, that the provision of tea (and coffee) was uppermost on the agenda. At a meeting held on 18 July 1771, the committee 'order'd that Mr Pritchard give orders to Farquaharsan & Cook for:

"'550 cups }
550 saucers } at 6d per piece

100 Basons pints at 16d d⁰
100 cups at 6d d⁰ "

and that:

"Mr B Laytor do provide
36 cups and saucers at 6½d a piece
60 d⁰ breakfast at 6½d a piece
200 coffee cups at 2/6 per dozen
150 breakfast Basons at 5d a piece
100 jugs for cream at 8d d⁰
50 jugs for d⁰ at 8d d⁰
100 brown Tea potts at 12d per doz"'

On 16 August, the committee ordered Messrs Cameron and Hogg to supply the Rooms with Tea 'agreeable to their proposals', and two weeks later, arranged for a bill for card- and tea-tables to be paid and ordered twelve more 'tea boards of the largest sizes'.

On 18 October 1771, it was 'Resolved that as the Major part of the Company have expressed their Desire that the Tea on the publick Ball Nights, may be paid for by every person that comes into the Rooms. The Managing Committee are come to a Resolution that each gentleman and Lady on a Ball Night are to pay sixpence on their admittance at the outward Door which will entice them to Tea.'

Tea sales obviously went well, for on 18 February 1772, Cameron and Hogg

Page from the minute book of the committee in charge of Bath Assembly Rooms, showing the entry for 18 July 1771 with a bulk order for teacups, basins, jugs and teapots.

were paid £98 18s 0d for tea, a further £48 8s 0d in May, and £46 for tea and coffee in December. By September 1772, the committee ordered '18 new large tea boards and 18 third size tea boards, 6 dozen small tea cups and saucers, 3 dozen large tea cups and saucers, and 2 dozen large tea pots'.

TEA FOR TRAVELLERS

Most travellers, when they keep diaries and travel journals, tend to record what they see *en route* and the nature of the places in which they stay rather than to keep a record of meals and drinks consumed. It is therefore difficult to build a clear picture of the sort of food and drink offered by landlords at coaching inns and taverns during the eighteenth century. A few invoices found in household accounts from the journey made in 1701 by the 2nd Duke and Duchess of Bedford from London to Chatsworth to visit the Duke's sister, the Duchess of Devonshire, show that they stayed overnight at an inn in Oxford. Their bill for supper on the day they arrived and dinner the following day lists what they and their servants ate: 'mutton, rabbits, onions and butter, chickens, guinea beans, artichokes, crayfish, cabbage, bacon and beans, veal, and quails'. They drank cider, mead, wine and milk, but there is no mention of tea or coffee.

But in 1775, when the Rev. James Woodforde set off for Bath, he recorded in his journal, 'We breakfasted at Burford, dined at Cirencester, and drank tea in the afternoon at the Cross Hands, and got into Bath about 8 o'clock in the evening. For breakfast, dinner, and tea in the afternoon, I paid £0 8s 0d.'

John Byng, Viscount Torrington, was an indefatigable traveller. A civil servant, he would spend his holidays in June and July each year visiting various parts of England and Wales, examining churches, old castles and private country houses. His diaries, kept in the 1780s, also indicate the wider availability of tea in inns all over Britain by the end of the century. It was while staying at the inn at Bagshot in 1782 that he recorded taking 'a pint of cream with my tea' at breakfast, and he also noted one day 'After tea, (which I sometimes allow myself on the road) ...'. Three years later, in Chipping Norton in Oxfordshire, he wrote, 'Here we came at ½ past six o'clock; after tea we endeavour'd to play at bowls in the garden.' Several of the receipts from the inns where he stayed have been preserved and so we know that at the Cross-Foxes in Mallwyd in Wales in July 1784, David Lloyd served him tea for 1s 4d; at Bala, Wales, on the same trip, John Jones at the Bull charged him 2s 4d for tea; at the Red Lion in Worksop in Nottinghamshire, his supper cost him 6s, his tea, 1s 6d, and his port and brandy a total of 6s 6d; at the Bull Inn in Horncastle, Lincolnshire in 1791, he paid 3s 6d for tea and coffee; and at the White Hart, Welwyn in Hertfordshire, in 1794, his tea cost him 2s 6d. At Wansford Bridge, Cambridgeshire, he wrote in his journal on Tuesday 29 June 1790, 'A good breakfast, with excellent tea; I seldom remark upon tea, but here every thing seems to be good.'

Tea was no longer an elegant upper-class beverage confined to the drawing rooms of society ladies. It was now a drink that everybody enjoyed at home, while travelling, at public places of entertainment – in fact, throughout Britain.

The Travellers' Breakfast, painted by Edward Villiers Rippingille, 1824. The figures depicted are members of the literary circle that surrounded Sir Charles Elton, including Coleridge, Southey, Dorothy and William Wordsworth. But the painting also shows the kind of breakfast offered at an inn, with the tea urn and cistern in the middle of the table.

TEA OR ALCOHOL?

With prices for tea still high, but the passion for drinking it growing, poets and essayists summed up many of the popular attitudes. There were many who praised tea, recommending it for health reasons, as Garway had done a hundred years before. Some pointed out its benefits as an alternative to alcohol. In 1708, in *The Lady's Last Stake*, Colley Cibber called it 'Thou soft, Thou sober, sage and venerable liquid', while Dr Nicholas Brady in *The Tea Table* (1724), wrote:

Hail Queen of Plants, Pride of Elysian Bowers!
How shall we speak thy complicated Pow'rs?
Thou wond'rous Panacea to asswage
The Calentures of Youth's fermenting rage,
And animate the freezing veins of age
...
Thus our Tea-Conversation we employ
Where with Delight, Instruction we enjoy;
Quaffing, without waste of Time or Wealth,
The Sov'reign Drink of Pleasure and of Health.

Duncan Campbell, in his *Poem Upon Tea*, 1735, praises tea as a far better choice than alcohol, especially for women, and wrote:

Tea is the Liquor of the Fair and Wise;
It chears the Mind without the least Disguise:
But Wine intoxicates, and wrongs each Sense;
Sweet innocent, mild Tea, gives no Offence:
It makes the Blood run sporting in the Veins,
Refines each Sense, and rectifies the Brains.

John Wesley, however, was initially totally against the use of tea. In his *Letter to a Friend Concerning Tea*, written in 1748, he pronounced that tea impaired the digestion, unstrung the nerves, involved great expense, and induced symptoms of paralysis. Although a tea drinker himself, he claimed that it made his hands shake and, in 1746, he called a meeting of his London Society of Methodists and put to them a proposal that they should give up tea for the sake of temperance. They all apparently followed his advice.

It is ironic therefore that in the next century tea was to become the symbol and focal point of the temperance movement, and John Wesley's Methodists the leading lights. Perhaps Wesley began to realise its benefits as an alternative to the copious amounts of gin and beer being consumed by the poor at this time, for in later life, he took up tea again and even organised tea drinkings for his ministers.

A late eighteenth-century temperance poster draws attention to the happy, healthy life to be had when tea replaces the evils of alcohol.

THE CONTRAST, Nº1. TEMPERANCE.

FURNITURE AND TEA WARES

By the early 1700s, the British East India Company was importing large quantities of porcelain from Japan and China along with teas, silks, rattan, cotton, spices, exotic woods, tortoiseshell and silver. In 1710, the Directors of the Company ordered its agents to send over '5,000 teapots with straight spouts, 5,000 small deep plates [stands] for the teapots, 8,000 milk pots, 2,000 small tea canisters, 3,000 sugar dishes, 3,000 bowls about 3 pint size, 12,000 boats [sic] for the teaspoons, 50,000 cups and saucers of the several patterns'. These were still not imported as 'sets', and traders (often called Chinamen and China-women) had to put sets together themselves. A line from the *Spectator* in 1712 quoted a typical retailer of the time, 'I am, dear Sir, one of the top China-women about town. One ... calls for a set of tea-dishes, another for a basin, a third for my best green tea.'

It was now possible to place orders for specific wares to be made and decorated in China and to ask for a special feature to be incorporated into the design – for example, a family coat of arms, a political symbol, an architectural drawing or a trade sign. In *Oriental Export Market Porcelain and its Influence on European Wares*, (1979), Geoffrey

Godden reports an eighteenth-century American traveller's description of how the Chinese industry worked, 'The chinaware is brought from the country [Ching-tê Chên – the centre inland for porcelain manufacture] plain, and painted according to fancy in the city [Canton]; they make us pay double price when they put a cypher on it, because they say it must go again into the kiln. They are great copyists and we have several sets of China to order with the family coat of arms.' The China Closet at Pollok House, just outside Glasgow, displays two armorial tea-sets made for Scottish families – one in 1750 for Lennox of Woodhead, and a second made for Thomas Bruce bearing the motto 'FUIMUS'.

Matching sets of tea wares began to arrive in large numbers in the 1770s. In 1775, the East India Company ordered '80 teasets' with their order for 1,200 teapots, 2,000 covered sugar bowls, 4,000 milk pots, 48,000 cups and saucers. These were often referred to as 'breakfast sets' and comprised a teapot, a sugar box with a cover and a plate for it to stand on, a milk pot, and twelve cups (still without handles) and saucers. Larger sets also included a second teapot, a slop basin and plate, a stand for the milk jug, a tea canister, and twelve coffee cups with handles, and sometimes a spoon tray and two plates for bread and butter.

Above: Pieces from a Chinese export porcelain tea service painted in red, black and gilt, dating from the 1720s or '30s. Each piece is decorated with the double-headed eagle of the Hoare family of Stourhead.

Left: Tea bowl and teapot, c.1800, from a oriental porcelain set in the Chinese Chippendale Bedroom at Saltram. The pieces are decorated in polychrome enamels with elaborately dressed figures and Chinese characters.

Above left: Teapot, tea caddy, slop dish and one teacup from a Worcester tea and coffee service, c.1770 at Saltram. Each piece was enamelled in London, and shows ruins of buildings and figures in green and black. The teacups and saucers are marked with crossed swords in imitation of Meissen.

Above right: A Furstenberg tea caddy, c.1770, decorated with oriental scenes, from Mrs Greville's collection of porcelain at Polesden Lacey.

Meanwhile, alongside the China trade, European potteries had started manufacturing large ranges of tea wares. In 1708 Augustus the Strong, Elector of Saxony, had established the Meissen porcelain factory which produced very fine copies of oriental wares. Inspired by Japanese Kakiemon and Imari porcelain teapot designs, they featured their distinctive bamboo, butterfly, bird, flower and foliage patterns in rich red, blue and yellow enamel. The Viennese and French manufacturers also produced porcelain tea wares, while the Italians concentrated more on coffee and chocolate cups and pots. When the Sèvres porcelain factory was established at the Palace of Vincennes in 1738, it produced no coffee or chocolate pots – only five different types of teapot. This is probably not an indication of which beverage the French were drinking at the time, but rather that the soft paste porcelain made at Sèvres was not suitable for the Continental method of keeping coffee hot over a burner. When the manufacture moved to a new building at Sèvres, in 1756, the focus continued on the production of tea-sets. Saucers tended to be larger than today, with a capacity to hold as much tea as the cup. Wealthy English families were important customers for these tea wares, and they often poured the tea into the saucer to cool it before drinking.

Many English potteries preferred not to risk money experimenting with the new methods, continuing to make teapots in earthenware and stoneware. In the 1750s, Josiah Wedgwood at his factory in Etruria in Staffordshire, perfected his 'creamware'. This achieved fame in 1765 when Queen Charlotte ordered a service and immediately asked for it to be named Queen's Ware. Gradually, however, the more enterprising manufacturers began to experiment with porcelain, at first on a small scale, and then with more confidence when they found that wealthy clients were prepared to pay large sums for the finer English tea wares. Pots, bowls, cups and saucers from companies like Worcester and Minton became readily available in England as alternatives to the imported oriental and European porcelains. In 1724, Daniel Defoe wrote in *A Tour thro' the Whole Island of Great Britain*, 'After we have passed Mile-End [to the east of the City of London], the village we come to is

Bow, where a large Manufactory of Porcelain is carried on. They have already made large Quantities of Tea-Cups, Saucers, Plates, Disches, Tureins, and most other Sorts of Useful Porcelain ... .'

At Stourhead, between 1779 and 1784, Sir Richard Hoare bought the following from Wedgwood and Bentley:

1779

1 Tea pot	3 6s 0d
1 Sugar dish	2 6s 0d
1 Slop Bason	1 6s 0d
3 small saucers	1 6s 0d
1 low cream ewer	1s 0d

1782

2 cream and sugar bowls	8s 0d
1 Tea pot	9d
4 Cups and Saucers	1s 0d
1 Slop Bason	2d
1 Sugar Dish	2d
1 Cream Jug	3d

1784

6 Breakfast basons and Saucers	15s 0d
6 Breakfast Cups and Saucers	9s 0d
8 coffee Cups and Saucers	12s 0d
6 chocolate Cups and Saucers	12s 0d
2 sugar basons	5s 0d
2 cream ewers	4s 0d
2 slop basons	4s 0d
2 muffin plates and water pans	13s 0d
1 large teapot	5s 6d
8 Bread and butter plates	16s 0d

As La Rochefoucauld pointed out, the possession of all these beautiful elegant tea wares and the serving of tea 'provides the rich with an opportunity to display their magnificence in the matter of tea-pots, cups and so on, which are always of most elegant design based upon Etruscan and other models of antiquity'.

Although by the 1750s and 1760s, tea was widely drunk amongst even the poorest families in Britain, their budget did not stretch to the purchase of fancy tea wares as well as the beverage itself. So, when poor folk organised a tea-party, they simply shared what they had. Jonas Hanway described how, in 1756, he had 'been told that in some places, where the people are so poor, that no one family possesses all the necessary apparatus for tea, they carry them to each others' houses to the distance of a mile or two, and club together materials for this fantastic amusement'. It seems that every social class, from those who lived in royal palaces to the very poorest country folk who struggled to make a living by menial labour, had its own set of rules and behaviour surrounding the ritual of tea drinking. By the end of the century, every house had its teapot, and no matter whether it was displayed in the elegant closet of a stately mansion or perched on the stone hearth of the open cottage fire, it was a vital piece of household equipment.

Georgian satirists loved to point up the difference in manners and style between the English and French. This cartoon, published in 1825, refers to the English custom of leaving a spoon either across or inside the teacup to show that the drinker did not require a refill. The unfortunate Frenchman, ignorant of this, has consumed thirteen cups of tea.

Wealthy families were also acquiring British or European silver tea wares, including urns which replaced large, cumbersome, heavy kettles in the 1760s, and these are recorded in many household accounts and inventories. At Dunham Massey in Cheshire, an inventory of silverware belonging to the 2nd Earl of Warrington, who died in 1758, included the following: tea-tables that sat on mahogany stands, three tea kettles with their own lamps and stands, two large waiters, four teapots and waiters, a hot water jug, three cream jugs, a sugar dish, a tea candlestick, and gilt tea canisters, sugar dishes, waiters for spoons, teaspoons, strainers and sugar tongs. This exhaustive list comes under the heading 'Tea Room' (see page 63), and also includes three green silk covers for the tea kettles.

Inventories for other properties record a similar story: at Lady Baillie's house, 'a yetlen kettle'; at Knole '6 small Teaspoons'; at Lord and Lady Audley's Cottage at Sandridge in Wiltshire 'One silver Tea Urn, 2 pr tea tongs, 20 tea spoons, 1 tea pot, 1 Tea Caddy'; at Kingston Hall 'a silver spout for a tea pott 3/6, a tea kettle 9/-'; at Woburn 'un pot a the', ordered and engraved with the family coat of arms in France, and various kettles, pots and stands with lamps; and at Dyrham Park 'a Tea Kittle with a lamp & frame and 1 tea pott'.

William Cowper's *The Task*, written in 1783, highlights the growing preference for the urn over the kettle:

Now stir the fire and close the shutter fast,
Let fall the curtains, wheel the sofa round
And while the bubbling and loud-hissing urn
Throws up a steamy column, and the cups
That cheer but not inebriate, wait on each,
So let us welcome peaceful evening in.

Teaspoons played a very important part in the etiquette of tea drinking. The Prince de Broglie recorded how he was taught the complexities of etiquette while on a visit to England in 1782: 'I partook of most excellent tea and I should be even now still drinking it, I believe, if the Ambassador had not charitably notified me at the twelfth cup that I must put my spoon across it when I wished to finish with this sort of warm water. He said to me: it is almost as ill-bred to refuse a cup of tea when it is offered to you, as it would [be] indiscreet for the mistress of the house to propose a fresh one, when the ceremony of the spoon has notified her that we no longer wish to partake of it.' This may have meant resting the spoon horizontally across the top of the cup or perhaps slanting it at an angle inside the cup.

The etiquette of tea drinking and the handling of tea wares in Scotland is illustrated in a poem written in 1810 by Sir Alexander Boswell, Esq of Auchinleck. Entitled *Edinburgh or The Ancient Royalty*, it refers to a typical scene in the previous century:

The chequer'd chairs, in seemly circle placed;
The Indian tray with Indian China graced;
The red stone Tea-pot with its silver spout;
The Tea Spoons numbered, and the tea fill'd out!

The spoons were numbered so that the hostess could ensure she returned the right cup to the right guest after refilling it. Boswell explained the etiquette of the second and third cup.

Hapless the wight, who, with lavish sup,
Empties too soon the Lilliputian cup!
Tho' patience fails, and tho' with thirst he urns,
All, all must wait till the last cup returns.
That cup returned, now see the hostess ply
The Tea-pot, measuring with equal eye,
To all again, at once she grants the boon,
Dispensing her gunpowder by platoon ...

As the ritual of tea drinking spread, so the demand for tea-tables also grew. To offer an alternative to the lacquer wares that were flooding into the country from the Far East, British cabinetmakers began to produce ornamental tea-tables in the early eighteenth century. William Blathwayt of Dyrham Park in Gloucestershire was a very successful civil servant, Secretary at War to William III, and as a consequence was able to observe the latest styles at the royal court. He furnished Dyrham with woods from the New World, and porcelain and tea furniture from the Far East. An inventory taken in 1703 lists a 'Japan Tea table and one Stand in the Plod Room', and a 'Large Tea Table and two Blacks' in the Balcony Room. Another inventory, taken seven years later, records further hand tea-tables. The inventory from 1725 for Canons in Middlesex, home of the Duke of Chandos, included 'a large Tea tables cover'd wth silver, in his Grace's Visiting room'. In 1740, the Duchess of Dorset at Knole was presented with a tea-table, a gold tea canister, a kettle and a lamp.

Tea and coffee were often also served on a silver 'waiter' (also called a 'salver' or 'table') which was then placed on top of a wooden stand. An inventory from Uppark in Sussex, written in 1722 on the death of Lord Tankerville, lists 'In my Lady's Bed Chamber & Closet a princess wood scritoir upon Drawers, an inlaid Table and stands, a Tea Table, a cain chair'. The two tables mentioned may well not have been tables with legs as we would understand today, but large trays that would be placed on the stands. Dunham Massey still has a pair of wooden tables made in 1741 and described as '2 mahogany stands to set the silver tea and coffee tables on'.

Left: Early eighteenth-century tea furniture in the Balcony Room at Dyrham Park. In the foreground is an oriental tea table, and behind, two candlestands supported by chained black slaves. The latter belonged to William Blathwayt's uncle, Thomas Povey, whose wealth was derived from administering Jamaican plantations.

Right: A set of Georgian tea containers in glass and silver, with their caddy, in the Green Drawing Room at Clandon Park in Surrey.

Cabinetmakers were fashioning wooden tea boxes to replace the porcelain jars that had first come from China during the previous century. The lockable chests contained two or three jars or boxes (for tea and sugar) which were made from crystal or silver. At Stourhead, Sir Richard Hoare paid £7 17s 6d for a 'neat Sattinwood Tea Chest banded with Tulipwood, lin'd with skyblue velvet, silver double bolted lock + 2 neatly cut oval glass Cannisters, with oval silver covers and Joints'. At Mount Stewart, displayed in the Drawing Room, is an eighteenth-century wooden caddy that belonged to Frances Anne, wife of the 3rd Marquess of Londonderry. It is decorated with chinoiserie motifs of ivory and contains three rectangular silver caddies. Chests like these were described in 1775 as 'a small kind of cabinet in which tea is brought to table'.

The fact that tea chests were always furnished with a sturdy lock reflects the high prices of the leaf. The brewing of it was never left to the servants but always carried out by the host or hostess, or one of their daughters – as La Rochefoucauld pointed out in 1784, 'It is also the custom for the youngest lady of the household to make the tea.' Jonathan Swift highlighted the lockable caddy in his satirical *Directions to Servants* published in 1745. In the chapter headed 'Advice to the Waiting Maid', he commiserates with her about the 'execrable Custom got among Ladies ... the Invention of small Chests and Trunks, with Lock and Key, wherein they keep the Tea and Sugar, without which it is impossible for the Waiting-maid to live. For, by this means, you are forced to buy brown Sugar, and pour Water upon Leaves, when they have lost all their Spirit and Taste.'

It seems the guardian of the caddy key carried it everywhere, even when away from home. William Cowper, while staying at the home of his friend Lady Hesketh in her absence, had to write to remind her that she had taken the key to her caddy away with her, thus committing her guest to days without a cup of tea! Mr E. Williams of Aberystwyth wrote in a letter to a friend at the beginning of the nineteenth century, 'My dear Friend, I am carried ... to the abbey by

Late eighteenth-century inlaid tea caddy from Fenton House. The inside is divided into four compartments, each lined with a metal called 'tea-pewter' made of a tin-lead alloy. Other woods used for chests and caddies included mahogany, fruit-wood, ebony, rosewood, burr yew and coromandel. Ornamentation was executed with inlaid woods or applied prints, or paper filigree decoration.

two gentlemen from Germany who are travelling in search of information ... they will take tea here and I suppose politeness will make it proper that I should tarry with them ... at all events I shall return as early as possible and enclose the key of my Tea Caddy and beg thee to direct my servants to provide Thee with Tea apparatus when I trust thou will feel thyself perfectly at home as I always wish thee to feel under my humble roof.'

Sending a boiler to a tea factory, Ceylon.

Above: Photograph, taken in the 1890s, showing an elephant train on its way to an up-country tea estate in Ceylon with a boiler made by Marshalls of Gainsborough in Lancashire.

Right: A public tea auction conducted in 1891, showing Ceylon tea being bought by the Mazawattee Tea Company for £25 10s per pound. In the late 1880s and early '90s, the British developed a craze for Ceylon teas from named estates and prices rocketed from £4–£5 per pound to £30–£36 15s. By December 1891, buyers and drinkers had realised the folly of paying such ridiculously high prices and the obsession with the very expensive Ceylon 'Golden Tips' evaporated almost overnight. More moderately priced Ceylon teas, however, continued to be extremely popular.

The Nineteenth Century

TEA FROM INDIA AND CEYLON

In the later eighteenth and early nineteenth centuries, Britain forged ahead of her European rivals as an industrial, technological and commercial nation. This remarkable achievement has been attributed by some historians to the fact that Britain was principally a tea-drinking nation, as opposed to the rest of coffee-drinking Europe. They argue that the widespread drinking of tea from the 1750s onwards contributed to the success of Britain's industrial revolution by safeguarding the health of a population that consumed a beverage made with boiled water, and was therefore less vulnerable to dysentery and other water-borne diseases. It is impossible to know if tea was indeed a contributing factor. Certainly it was firmly established by the mid-eighteenth century as the British beverage but the amounts consumed were not enormous. Prices remained high for another hundred years, due to taxation, while consumption per head actually fell.

Rather than crediting tea with speeding industrial advancement, it could be argued that Britain's fondness actually diminished the energies of the working classes, because they preferred to pay for a beverage that offered little nutrition instead of buying 'proper' foods.

But cheaper tea was on its way. Until 1834 all tea coming into Britain was from China, carried only in East India ships: the Company had partially lost its monopoly in 1813 but managed to fend off competition for a further twenty years. At the same time, trouble was brewing between Britain and China concerning the opium trade. Britain was spending vast amounts of silver on the purchase of tea because there were few goods that the Chinese wanted in return. What they did want was opium, an illegal but widely-used drug. The East India Company was growing opium in its territories in eastern India, and trading it to China via wholesalers in Calcutta. In 1839 the Chinese Emperor decided to end this trade, ordering twenty thousand chests containing opium to be deposited on the beach so that the sea would wash it away. The following year, the British declared war on China, who retaliated by placing an embargo on tea exports.

Meanwhile the East India Company had been searching for new territory in India in which to grow tea. As early as 1788, the tea plant had been discovered growing wild in the north-eastern state of Assam, but it was not until the 1820s that serious discussion took place as to whether this would be a viable area for production. After years of trials, the first Assam tea reached the London auctions in 1839, and new plantations were subsequently laid out in various regions of India. In the 1860s, the industry was established in Ceylon, and tea from the British estates became very popular. Imaginative advertising and attractive packaging from such companies as Lipton, Mazawattee, Ridgways, Brooke Bond and Teetgen pushed Ceylon teas to the forefront of the market.

The amount of tea imports from India and Ceylon rose rapidly over the next thirty years. Whereas in 1866 Britain imported 97,681,000 pounds from China compared to 4,584,000 from India, by 1896 the comparisons were 24,549,936 from China, 122,941,000 from India, and 80,294,474 from Ceylon. The black teas from the British territories were obviously cheaper, and welcomed by the home market. By the end of the century, Britain had become a nation of almost exclusively black tea drinkers.

TEA BY CLIPPER SHIP

Until the end of the East India Company's monopoly, tea was brought to Britain on board the company's own sailing ships or on vessels hired to them. Slowed down by the weight of their huge cargoes, these East Indiamen took from ten to fifteen months to make the journey. No other ships were permitted to carry tea into London's docks.

Once the monopoly was broken in 1834, it became legal for other companies to ship tea, though the British Navigation Laws allowed only British ships to trade between China and the United Kingdom. Despite the Boston Tea Party, there was a thriving demand for tea in the United States, and American shippers could now exploit both their own trade and the routes from the Far East to European ports. In 1845 the first of the American clippers was launched and made the round trip from New York to China and back in less than eight months. When the Navigation Laws were repealed in 1849, American shippers took full advantage of the new opportunities in the British market. To combat the onslaught, the first British clipper, the *Stornaway*, was built in Aberdeen in 1850. Some British companies had their clippers built in America, and one of these, the *Lightning*, logged an average speed of eighteen

knots, a record for a sailing ship.

The clippers were built like sleek yachts, with elaborate decoration and graceful lines, but capable of carrying more than a million pounds of tea. The chests, packed intricately by Chinese stevedores, and the stolidity of stowage helped to give the ships added stability and strength, increasing their performance and ability to withstand fast currents, monsoon tides, gales and the dangers posed by reefs on the homeward voyage. Soon these fast ships were racing each other to be first to land the new season's teas in the port of London.

Canton had for a long time been the most important Chinese port for the export of tea and remained so until the 1850s. Ships were loaded at Whampoa, on an island in the Pearl River about ten miles below Canton and 60 miles from the open sea. Shanghai was also an important port, but when the shipping agents discovered that tea was available earlier at Fouchow (the main port for Fukien Province) the focus for the clipper companies changed. Teas picked and manufactured in Fukien in the early spring were ready for loading in Fouchow in the middle of June whereas Shanghai and Canton did not have their teas until five or six weeks later. If a particular ship was to be the first into London, these time differences really mattered.

As soon as the clippers were loaded, they set sail for home, sometimes not even completing the official paperwork for fear of losing precious time. Several ships would leave on the same tide but no one knew who would win the race until the first had sailed past Gravesend into the Thames estuary. The dealers in London were prepared. The sampling clerks often spent the previous night in hotels in the capital or even slept at the docks in order to be available to taste and evaluate the cargo as soon as it had been landed. Telegrams recorded arrival times as the individual ships sailed past certain marker points. For the general public, this was like following the Derby, and for a few days the race became the main topic of conversation in clubs and drawing rooms. Crowds gathered to see the ships dock and the cargo tossed on to the dockside. Samples were in the tasting rooms by 9am, and once the dealers had placed their bids and the sales transactions had been completed, the chests of tea were quickly transported all over Britain so that customers could buy their own samples of the new season's teas. The members of the crew of the winning ship were paid £500 by the owners of the cargo, for the first tea home fetched at least 3d to 6d a pound higher than cargoes on board subsequent ships to reach home.

The most exciting of the races ended in a dead heat between *Ariel and Taeping* on 7 September 1866. Three years later, the Suez Canal opened, steam became more important than sail and the clippers were doomed. But for those 20 years or so, the clipper races had gained more publicity for tea than any advertising by individual companies.

Poster advertising tea from the great clipper race of 1866. Eleven clippers set off from Fouchow in May, and four, Taeping, Ariel, Fiery Cross *and* Serica *raced almost neck and neck until they entered the English Channel. The final part of the race was between* Ariel *and* Taeping, *and ended ninety-nine days after leaving China, when* Taeping *berthed just twenty minutes ahead. The owners of the two clippers agreed to settle for a dead heat.*

GREAT RACE
OF THE
TEA SHIPS,
WITH THE FIRST
NEW SEASON'S TEAS.

PRICE OF TEAS REDUCED.

THE "Taeping," "Ariel," "Fiery Cross," and "Serica" have arrived, with others in close pursuit, with something like FORTY-FIVE MILLION POUNDS OF NEW TEA on board—half a year's consumption for the United Kingdom. This enormous weight coming suddenly into the London Docks, Shippers are compelled to submit to MUCH LOWER PRICES, in order to make sales.

We are thus enabled to make a Reduction of FOURPENCE in the pound.

4/0 down to - - 3/8
3/8   „   - - 3/4
3/4   „   - - 3/0
And so on downwards.

We may add the above Ships have brought a few lots of most unusual fine quality.

Reduction takes place on Friday the 21st inst.

135, OXFORD STREET;
57, STRETFORD ROAD; and
171, STRETFORD ROAD—
"Great Northern."

BURGON & CO.,
TEA MERCHANTS.

Giant storage tins of Hyson tea amongst other goods in the dry storage room, running off the housekeeper's room at Wimpole Hall in Cambridgeshire. Like the smaller caddies kept in the drawing room, these tins were locked firmly against possible pilfering by servants.

TEA FOR SALE

From 1833 onwards, all Britain's ports were open to the China trade, enabling merchants to land tea and to trade where they wished. Although London continued to have the entire country as its potential market, companies in each region developed their own trading areas and patterns according to local preferences and demands.

Brooke Bond started trading in Manchester, Liptons in Glasgow, John Horniman introduced his idea of packaging tea from south London, Harrison and Crossfield were based in Liverpool, Priory Tea traded from Birmingham, and the English & Scottish Joint Cooperative Wholesalers Society was established by a group of weavers in Rochdale in Lancashire. But traders recognised that high taxation directly affected consumption, and consequently their sales, so they strove to convince the government to reduce the burden of tea duty. In 1846, a society of Liverpool merchants declared the tax 'exorbitant, impolitic, and oppressive'. A letter was sent to Sir Robert Peel, the Tory Prime Minister, to argue, 'that the duties have been imposed without any reference to the encouragement of its consumption; that the quantity required by the public for their wants and comfort has never entered into the considerations of the legislature; that all they have looked to has been to get a certain amount of revenue from tea, treating it, important as it is to the people's sustenance and well-being, as a subject unworthy of consideration, *per se*, and for their benefit ...'. The merchants threw in the additional claims that if the tea tax were to be reduced, less alcohol would be consumed, fewer crimes would be committed and people would live longer in better health.

In 1852 Benjamin Disraeli proposed a reduction of the duty to one shilling per pound over six years, but he was opposed by his great rival, William Gladstone, and the tax remained at 2s 2¼d per pound. However, when Gladstone came to power the following year, he proposed the same changes, going further in 1863 to cut the tax to one shilling per pound, and in 1865 to sixpence. This eventual reduction meant that, by the time Julius Drewe set up the Willow Pattern Tea Store in Liverpool in 1878, consumption was increasing. In 1885 he opened a chain of Home & Colonial Stores, and made tea the most important product, selling the highest quality Indian teas for the smallest profit margin. Within a year, he owned four large stores and nine smaller branches and by 1890, there were 43 branches dotted around Britain. Another grocery magnate, Thomas Lipton,

introduced Ceylon tea to his chain of 300 stores in the 1890s, winning prizes for its quality at the Chicago World's Fair in 1893. Like Julius Drewe, he offered his teas to the British public at lower prices than ever before, sold massive amounts and rapidly became a multimillionaire.

Even women involved themselves in this aspect of business – either working alongside their husbands or setting up their own tea firms. In Mrs Gaskell's *Cranford*, published in 1853, Miss Matty, a genteel lady fallen upon hard times, is persuaded to become a dealer in tea. 'Why should not Miss Matty sell tea – be an agent to the East India Tea Company which then existed? I could see no objections to this plan, while the advantages were many – always supposing that Miss Matty could get over the degradation of condescending to anything like trade. Tea was neither greasy, nor sticky – grease and stickiness being two of the qualities which Miss Matty could not endure.'

As well as specialist tea dealers, other traders, such as grocers, chemists, confectioners and department stores, also included tea among the goods that they stocked. In 1872, the London Genuine Tea Company invited sub-postmasters to act as their agents and postmen to sell teas from door to door. All the companies, both old and new, grew and flourished as

customers' requirements increased. A typical tea drinker, Colonel Chichester, bought his tea from a number of different merchants such as Twinings, who boasted a long list of noble clients including Queen Victoria (who granted Richard Twining a Royal Warrant in 1837, the first year of her reign), Fortnum & Company, 'Tea Dealers and Grocers' in Piccadilly, and Lanson & Simpson of Blackfriars in London.

The 1840s publication, *Tea and the Tea Trade*, written by a London brokerage house, looked at the growth in consumption 'from a very few pounds, till it has reached the astonishing extent of twenty-five millions per annum, and probably it is capable of being carried still further. It may be literally said to have descended from the palace to the cottage, and from a fashionable and expensive luxury, has been converted into an essential comfort, if not an absolute necessity of life.' It goes on to examine the economic significance for Britain: 'What yields a revenue to our govenment of five millions and a half per annum? – Tea. What article in the grocery business pays for all the loss of bad debts, etc – Tea. What has made some of our London bankers? What has made some Members of Parliament? – Retailing of Tea. What has enabled others to purchase landed estates? – Retailing of Tea.'

The fact that so many companies were now trading tea meant that advertising and publicity were extremely important if a business was to keep existing customers and gain the loyalty of new ones. David Lewis's Department Store in Birmingham started selling tea in 1886, and in an advertisement in the *Illustrated London News*, it explained how this came about:

Lewis's have not always sold tea, but having a very large number of employees to provide with an afternoon meal, Lewis's was struck with the difficulty of procuring a good, drinkable refreshing tea for them at a moderate price. The ordinary teas were perfectly abominable. Tired of the constant and not unreasonable complaints of the perpetual changing of their tea-dealers, Lewis's had at last resolved to buy their tea for the use of the establishment, direct from the shippers. They began to sell tea to their friends, and at last were induced to make the sales public in Lancashire, where they now sell twenty thousand pounds of tea a week. Lewis's now feel that they have benefited only a small proportion of the population; they intend in future to make their tea known all over the United Kingdom.

By 1890, they had fulfilled their ambition. Their two-shilling packets of tea were indeed known throughout the land.

Twinings used the fact that they were 'suppliers to the nobility and gentry' to encourage sales. Thomas Lipton added the slogan 'Direct from the Tea Gardens to the Tea Pot' to his colourful packets and adverts. He then instructed his tasters to create blends that suited the different water in the various parts of Britain and, with the slogan 'The perfect tea to suit the water of your own town', he made sure he was one step ahead of the rest. Priory Tea hired a hot-air balloonist to fly over Birmingham and drop leaflets saying, 'Priory Tea – Best Value in the World. This handbill was dropped from the skies by Lieutenant Lemprière, navigating The Golden Eagle Balloon. June 16th 1894.'

Advertisers had no qualms about using the royal family and leading members of society to endorse their products. This advertisement for Avoncherra tea shows Gladstone's Cabinet Council of 1892, with all members drinking their cup of tea. The second person seated on the right is Sir George Otto Trevelyan of Wallington. Following in the footsteps of the ardent teetotaller, Sir Walter Calverley Trevelyan, he campaigned to control the sale of alcohol, arguing that it was a principal cause of poverty.

Nineteenth-century advertisements for Mazawattee tea. The snappy trademark of the company was created in 1886 when the Hindu mazatha (luscious) was combined with the Cingalese wattee (garden or plant growth). The company recognised the importance of eye-catching advertising and was one of the first to use large enamelled signs on buildings and railways stations. Members of the family who owned the company posed for some of the advertisements, such as the famous 'Old Folks at Home'.

Every effort was made by tea companies to sell their produce. Special blends were created for members of the royal family and their images added to advertisements. Poems and songs, special offers and competitions all encouraged the public to buy more packets. Other products, such as sugar, were sold as loss-leaders, and teapots, pianos, household linens, and even pensions were offered as free gifts in exchange for coupons or labels. *Woman's Weekly* for 11 March 1899 ran a brief article entitled 'All with a Pound of Tea':

Particulars of an interesting pension scheme for widows, started by an enterprising Lincolnshire firm of tea merchants, have been sent to the Daily Chronicle by a clergyman, who remarks that 'it looks to me too good to be true.'

Every married woman, it seems, who purchases half a pound of their tea weekly for five consecutive weeks is entitled to a pension of 10s a week in the event of her husband dying, provided he was in good health when she commenced buying the tea, such pension to be continued so long as she remains a widow.

Lewis's Department Store included these lines in their advertising tea poem:

A tea beneficial, of beautiful blend;
A tea mild and mellow that none can mend;

A tea strong and savoury, lasting and luscious;
A national tea, tea quite nutritious;
A capital tea, choice too, and cheerful,
The price of it, too, is not at all fearful
But reasonable, radical, rare and right,
Selling fast from morn till late at night.
Famous and fashionable, faultless and fine,
Drinks richer by far than the richest of wine.

Charles Dickens described how Little Dorrit would walk with Maggy, but the latter 'must stop at a grocer's window, short of their destination, for her to show her learning. She stumbles through various philanthropic recommendations to Try our Mixture, Try our Family Black, Try our Orange-flavoured Pekoe, challenging competition at the head of Flowery Teas; and various cautions to the public against spurious establishments and adulterated articles.'

By the 1870s and 1880s, the 'adulterated articles' were less in evidence. As prices dropped, so the practice by unscrupulous British traders of mixing tea with the leaves of other plants gradually died out. By avoiding Chinese green and black teas, and by buying only black leaf from the British plantations in India and Ceylon, two things were ensured – a lower price and

unadulterated tea. In 1870, the *Grocer's Manual* observed:

the green Teas (Twankey, Hyson and Gunpowder), as well as Black Bohea Tea, so popular forty or fifty years ago, are now seldom heard of: and indeed a great portion of what now comes from China is tea-dust, which is mostly used in mixing with Indian and Ceylon growth. It has been found that these latter, especially Assam teas, are nearly twice as strong as Chinese sorts. The public seems to like 'strong' teas better than weak thin kinds, however fragrant; and a rasping, pungent Indian Pekoe Souchong, and a thick, strong, broken Pekoe, pleases the working classes better than a choice Darjeeling tea worth four times as much.

It is fascinating that the preference for strong pungent tea in nineteenth-century Britain is still so much in evidence in the first years of the twenty-first.

TEA FOR BREAKFAST

For those who enjoyed a comfortable lifestyle, breakfast in the early days of the nineteenth century was eaten at about 10am and usually consisted of tea, coffee or chocolate, with bread or toast and butter. Georgiana Caroline Sitwell remembered that at her family's home, Renishaw, in Derbyshire, 'the hours of meals were rather later than at most other country houses. Breakfast from 1826–1846 was nominally at ten, but often did not begin until eleven o'clock.... Breakfast comprised only tea and toast, with an egg for the elder people if they desired it.'

Later in the century, 8 or 8.30am was the preferred time in most households for a breakfast that became much more substantial – especially for men who needed a hearty meal before setting off for the office ready for a 9am start to the working day. Mrs Isabella Beeton's Bills of Fare in her 1861 *Book of Household Management* suggested

any cold meat the larder may furnish, should be nicely garnished, and be placed on the buffet. Collared and potted meats or fish, cold game or poultry, veal-and-ham pies, game-and-rumpsteak pies, are all suitable dishes for the breakfast table; as also cold ham, tongue, etc, etc. The following list of hot dishes may perhaps assist our readers in knowing what to provide.... Broiled fish, such as mackerel, whiting, herrings, dried haddocks, etc... mutton chops and rump steaks, broiled sheep's kidneys, kidneys à la maître d'hôtel, sausages, plain rashers of bacon, bacon and poached eggs, ham and poached eggs, omelets, plain boiled eggs, oeufs-au-plat, poached eggs on toast, muffins, toast, marmalade, butter, etc. etc.

When Swiss chef Gabriel Tschumi took up his post at Windsor Castle, he was very surprised 'to find that breakfast was as big a meal as the main meal of the day in Switzerland'. Going down to the kitchens on his first morning, he assumed:

as lunch and dinner were meals of about eight courses, breakfast would be a very light meal indeed. I found instead, that the coal ranges were red-hot and the spits packed with chops, cutlets, steaks, bloaters, sausages, chicken and woodcock. The roast chefs were deftly removing them and piling them onto huge platters. In other parts of the kitchen cooks were trimming rashers of streaky bacon, a quarter of an inch thick, for grilling, and preparing egg dishes.... I asked how many different dishes were served to the Royal Family for breakfast. 'Five' came the reply.

Hearty breakfasts continued to feature in wealthy households. A visitor to Knightshayes Court, the Devon home of the Heathcoat Amory family, in the first years of the twentieth century recalled the breakfast sideboard. 'On a hunting day it was such fun ... the sideboard loaded with cold ham, galantine and other meats, sliced bread and a pile of grease-proof paper and you went and made your own sandwiches ....'

The first *National Food Inquiry* of 1863 discovered that little had changed for the working classes since the late eighteenth century and that farm labourers and home workers, such as silk weavers, needlewomen, glove makers and shoemakers, throughout Britain, started the day with a meagre meal of milk or water gruel or porridge, bread and butter, and tea. Tea was for most people the preferred breakfast drink. Charles Dickens's David Copperfield describes how 'Miss Murdstone took Dora's arm in hers, and marched us into breakfast as if it were a soldier's funeral. How many cups of tea I drank, because Dora made it, I don't know. But I perfectly remember that I sat swilling tea until my whole nervous system, if I had any in those days, must have gone by the board.'

There were of course many in society who did not have a comfortable dining room in which to take breakfast.

Dickens's stories are full of poor families, young apprentices, social outcasts, and those who survived from hand to mouth, just about coping in very mean lodgings that contrast markedly with the sumptuous breakfast tables of the upper and middle classes. For them, 'public houses will either send tea and bread and butter

.... for breakfast, or provide it for him at the house'. Recording his impressions of England in 1809, the Swedish visitor Erik Gurstat Geijer wrote 'One may see in many places small tables set up under the open sky, round which coal carters and workmen empty their cups of this delicious beverage.'

Martha Chute, who lived at The Vyne in Hampshire in the mid-nineteenth century, painted a series of charming watercolours of daily life there. This painting, c.1860, shows the dining-room table set for breakfast with the teacups arranged to flank the tea urn.

French visitors found the after-dinner habits of the English particularly peculiar. These two illustrations, engraved by a French prisoner of war in 1814, shows the men at table, drinking their wine and trying to piss into chamber pots, while the women and children sit solemnly around the tea urn in the drawing room, with a black servant handing around the teacups.

TEA AFTER DINNER

Dinner had been gradually pushed to a later and later slot in the day – from 4 or 5pm in the 1780s and 1790s to 7.30 or 8pm in the 1850s. This left a long gap between breakfast and the main meal of the day and so a new meal was created. 'Luncheon' or 'nuncheon' had developed from the eighteenth-century 'nunchin' – defined in Dr Johnson's dictionary in 1755 as 'a piece of victuals eaten between meals'. Jane Austen speaks of 'noonshine' in 1808, and by 1832, 'to lunch' had become an accepted verb. Georgiana Sitwell recorded that in the 1840s, 'luncheon was at two and in 1834, dinner at half-past six, though in Derbyshire six o'clock seems to have been more usual'. In 1861, Mrs Beeton was recommending 'the remains of cold joints, nicely garnished, a few sweets, or a little hashed meat, poultry or game ... with bread and cheese, biscuits, butter, etc .... In families where there is a nursery, the mistress of the house often partakes of the meal with the children .... And makes it her luncheon.'

In upper-class homes, tea was still an after-dinner beverage taken in the drawing room in the late afternoon or early evening. Several of Jane Austen's novels include scenes that centre around the ritual. In *Sense and Sensibility*, Elinor attends a social gathering at Lady Middleton's, eager to have a chat with Lucy, but 'the insipidity of the meeting was exactly such as Elinor had expected; it produced not one novelty of thought or expression; and nothing could be less interesting than the whole of their discourse both in the dining-parlour and drawing room ... they quitted it only with the removal of the tea things'.

The ceremonial brewing of the tea continued to take place in the drawing room. A servant would carry in all the tea equipage and any food to be offered, but would leave the lady or daughter of the house actually to brew and serve the tea. In *Mansfield Park*, Jane Austen wrote, 'The next opening of the door brought something more welcome; it was the tea things ... Susan and an attendant girl ... brought in everything necessary for the meal ....'

Because of the expense involved in offering tea to callers, Mrs Gaskell's working-class characters in Manchester only occasionally invited friends around for tea in the early evening. In *Mary Barton*, written in 1848 before 'afternoon tea' had really become a social institution, Alice Wilson met Mary in the street one day and 'ventured to ask her if she would come in and take tea with her that very evening ... she borrowed a cup; of odd saucers she had plenty ... half an ounce of tea and a quarter of a pound of butter went far to absorb her morning wages ....'

Even towards the end of the nineteenth century, in some households tea was still served after dinner in the traditional way. As late as 1889, *Good Form, a book of everyday etiquette* by Mrs Armstrong instructed that at the end of dinner, 'Before the host leaves the dining-room, he should ring the bell for tea, which is brought into the drawing-room as soon as the gentlemen have returned. A little music is generally given after dinner and the guests begin to leave about half-past ten.'

AFTERNOON TEA, A NATIONAL INSTITUTION

THE 'INVENTION' OF AFTERNOON TEA

It is impossible to pinpoint exactly when tea was first served as an afternoon event that took place between midday luncheon and evening dinner. Routines varied greatly between city and country, between classes, and depending on each individual day's activities. But there is no doubt that some time in the late 1830s and early 1840s, the taking of tea in the afternoon developed into a new social event. Jane Austen hints at it as early as 1804 in an unfinished novel about a family called the Watsons. One scene shows that evening entertainments still featured a tea room for refreshments: 'At the end of the dances, Emma found they were to drink tea …. The tea-room was a small room within the card-room'. A later episode, however, tells us that dinner for at least some people was now taken much later. When Tom Musgrave made a visit to the Watsons, before 'going home to an eight o'clock dinner', he was surprised to be shown into the best parlour where 'he beheld a circle of smart people … arranged with all the honours of visiting round the fire, and Miss Watson seated at the best

Pembroke table, with the best tea-things before her'. Almost certainly after-dinner tea drinking for the Watsons, but coming between luncheon and dinner for him.

Dinner and tea now exchanged places. The accepted tea legend always attributes the 'invention' of afternoon tea to Anna Maria, wife of the 7th Duke of Bedford, who wrote to her brother-in-law in a letter sent from Windsor Castle in 1841: 'I forgot to name my old friend Prince Esterhazy who drank tea with me the other evening at 5 o'clock, or rather was my guest amongst eight ladies at the Castle.' The Duchess is said to have experienced 'a sinking feeling' in the middle of the afternoon, because of the long gap between luncheon and dinner and so asked her maid to bring her all the necessary tea things and something to eat – probably the traditional bread and butter – to her private room in order that she might stave off her hunger pangs.

The actress Fanny Kemble described in a footnote to a letter written on 27 March 1842 how her first intro-duction to afternoon tea took place at Belvoir Castle in Rutland, where she and the Duchess of Bedford were house guests. 'I received on several occasions private and rather mysterious invitations to the Duchess of Bedford's room, and found her with a "small and select" circle of female guests of the castle, busily

employed in brewing and drinking tea, with her grace's own private tea kettle.' She added, 'I do not believe that the now universally honoured and observed institution of five-o'clock tea dates further back in the annals of English civilisation than this very private and, I think, rather shamefaced practice of it.' A visitor to the Duchess's own home, Woburn Abbey, in the 1840s explained how she had a tea room where she was to be found 'from five o'clock to half past, and where you may refresh yourself on arriving (as I did)'.

Certainly Georgiana Sitwell wrote quite categorically of the 1830s,

There was no gathering for five o'clock afternoon tea in those days, but most ladies took an hour's rest in their rooms before the six or seven o'clock dinner, retiring thither with their books …. It was not till about 1849 or 50, … that five o'clock tea in the drawing room was made an institution, and then only in a few fashionable houses where the dinner hour was as late as half past seven or eight o'clock. My mother was the first to introduce the custom to Scotland; and this was in consequence of Lord Alexander Russell, who was staying with us at Balmoral, telling her that his mother, the Duchess of Bedford, always had afternoon tea at Woburn.

The Trevelyan family holding a tea-party in the Central Hall at Wallington, 1899. The menu for such a tea would have included scones, muffins, tea cakes, various biscuits or shortbreads, and large cakes – almond, gingerbread, madeira, simnel, chocolate – and small cakes such as eclairs, cream jumbles and macaroons.

Teatime in a poor Victorian household. In his book, Tea: its Mystery and History, *1878, Samuel Phillips Day wrote 'what was first regarded as a luxury, has now become, if not an absolute necessity, at least one of our accustomed daily wants…. Consumed by all classes, serving not simply as an article of diet, but as a refreshing and invigorating beverage, tea cannot be too highly estimated.'*

Manners of Modern Society, written in 1872, described the way in which afternoon tea had gradually become an established event. 'Little Teas', it explained, 'take place in the afternoon' and were so-called because of the small amount of food served and the neatness and elegance of the meal. They were also known as 'Low Teas', because guests were seated in low armchairs with low side-tables on which to place their cups and saucers, 'Handed Teas', since the hostess handed round the cups, and 'Kettledrums', presumably because the kettle was a vital piece of equipment

involved in the ceremony. The book continued, 'Now that dinners are so late, and that "teas proper" [that is, after-dinner tea as it was taken in the earlier part of the century] are postponed in consequence to such an unnatural hour as ten p.m; The want is felt of the old-fashioned meal at five, and so it has been reinstated, though not quite in the same form as before.'

Diaries, journals and memoirs from the second half of the century are full of tea. The diaries of Augusta, Viscountess Middleton, are typical. In 1855, tea features hardly at all, by 1862 there are regular references to tea at home and tea taken in other people's homes, and in 1870, almost every day seems to have involved a tea-party or gathering of some description.

By the end of the century, afternoon tea had crossed all class barriers. Even in small villages and hamlets, what was referred to by some as 'visitor's tea' was a more refined occasion than most cottage meals. In her autobiographical account of her late nineteenth-century childhood in an Oxfordshire village, *Lark Rise to Candleford*, Flora Thompson describes tea with Mrs Herring: 'the table was laid … there were the best tea things with a fat pink rose on the side of each cup; hearts of lettuce, thin bread and butter, and the crisp little cakes that had been baked in readiness that morning. Edmund and Laura (then young children) sat very upright on their hard Windsor chairs.'

Flora Thompson describes too how more impromptu tea gatherings were a regular event for the village women:

Those of the younger set ... would sometimes meet in the afternoon in one of their cottages to sip strong, sweet, milkless tea and talk things over. These tea-drinkings were never premeditated. One neighbour would drop in, then another, and another would be beckoned to from the doorway or fetched in to settle some disputed point. Then someone would say, 'How about a cup o' tay?' And they would all run home to fetch a spoonful, with a few leaves over to help make a spoonful for the pot.... This tea-drinking time was the woman's hour.

In Wales, the village women formed Tea Clubs or Clwb Tê and, as in earlier times when money was short, the equipment and the food and drink needed was pooled. As Marie Trevelyan explained in 1893, 'One woman would bring tea, one a cake, another a drop of gin or brandy to put in it. They visited the homes of the members in turn, and naturally gossiped about what interested women.'

The writer George Gissing summed up the social role of tea when he wrote at the end of the century, 'Nowhere is the English genius of domesticity more notably evident than in the festival of afternoon tea. The mere chink of cups and saucers tunes the mind to happy repose.'

Women in traditional Welsh costume, Llandudno, c.1900. Marie Trevelyan wrote in 1893: 'the hill women [of Wales] are fond of drinking tea in immoderate quantities.... The teapot is always on the hob, there is no end to the potations. There is no limit to the sippings.'

TEA-PARTIES FOR ALL OCCASIONS

The 1879 edition of Mrs Beeton's *Book of Household Management* described high teas, afternoon teas with bread and butter, little teas for the family, and 'a veritable tea-party, such as our Grandmothers delighted to give'. These, it said, 'are far from unfashionable – the repast differs little from the family one ... only that there would be extra provision made and, probably, more attention bestowed upon it'. By 'Grandmothers' teas', she presumably meant 'afternoon tea' as taken by the Duchess of Bedford.

The Tea and Chatter column for December 1890 in *Beauty & Fashion* reported: 'smaller "tea fights" have been largely eclipsed for the last three or four seasons by the more attractive "At Homes"; and instead of five o'clock tea meetings, the custom, now, is to drop in any time between four and seven, when the kettle will be boiling.... Seven o'clock is on the verge of striking before the rooms are cleared, and then very often the hostess breathes a sigh of relief and hurries away to dress for a dinner party or the theatre.'

'At Home' teas and 'Tea Receptions' were large afternoon events for up to two hundred guests. Tea was laid out on a large table in the corner of the drawing or dining room, and servants would be on hand to pour and hand round the cups of tea, sugar, cream or milk, cakes, and bread and butter. Sometimes, as Mrs Beeton suggested, the hostess would organise 'some entertainment ... usually music, professional singers and pianists being sometimes engaged'. Mrs Armstrong in *Good Form*, 1889, explains 'Afternoon dances are seldom given in town, but they form a popular kind of entertainment at military stations, and during the yachting season at Cowes.' At such events 'refreshments are going on all the afternoon, and the gentlemen take the ladies to the tea-room during intervals between the dances'.

London society also enjoyed what were called 'Drawing Room Teas'. These were held in the houses of ladies who attended Queen Victoria's receptions or 'Drawing Rooms' at Buckingham Palace. After the royal reception was over, a favoured few of the ladies of the court went to the home of one of their number for tea. As Mrs Armstrong describes the scene: 'The room is soon full of ladies in their court dresses, each carrying her bouquet of flowers, and her train over her left arm. The hostess enters, looking the best of all, and passes about the room, greeting her guests. The room is full of shimmering silks and brocades ... the ladies are surrounded by groups of worshippers, and each one is entreated in turn to let down her train so as to display the full beauty of her attire'. Tea for such events (also called 'train teas' on account of the long trains that were a part of typical court dresses and which had to be managed with great care if ladies were not to trip or stumble while curtseying) was laid in another room, and followed the pattern of a tea at an ordinary 'At Home'.

Engraving from the Graphic, *showing a 'Kettledrum in Knightsbridge', 1871. The caption reads 'In this form of afternoon party, ladies and gentlemen can mingle. "Tea in the arbour", which used to be reckoned among the vulgarities, has got into society: it is certainly much better to talk scandal in the garden than indoors.'*

THE ETIQUETTE OF AFTERNOON TEA

Tea drinking no longer took place in private boudoirs and small withdrawing rooms, but in the hall, the centre of the Victorian home, where games were played, parties organised and afternoon tea taken. When Standen in Sussex was designed by the architect Philip Webb as a country house for James and Margaret Beale and their seven children, he took into account the fact that on cold and wet days tea would be taken in the hall. Even so, as the children grew up and married, more space had to be provided for these gatherings. In 1898 Webb was asked to add a bay window and alcove.

Invitations to tea were issued verbally or by a small informal note or card. Etiquette writers advised that 'no answer is necessary. When the day arrives, if you are disengaged, and so disposed, you call upon your friend'. Several nineteenth-century writers on etiquette gave their recommendations as to the correct time for afternoon tea. In 1884, Marie Bayard advised in *Hints on Etiquette* that 'the proper time ... is from four to seven', whereas others advised 'about five', or referred to 'small 5 o'clock teas'. Guests were not expected to stay for the entire time that tea was going on, but to come and go as they pleased during the allotted hours. Most stayed half an hour or an hour but 'should on no account stay later than seven o'clock'. *The Lady at Home and Abroad*, 1898, explained the different ways of receiving guests. For small teas, 'the hostess receives her friends in the drawing room as on any other afternoon ... but when it is a case of a regular afternoon entertainment, she stands at the head of the staircase and receives as she would at a ball or a wedding reception'.

Mrs Armstrong's *Good Form* explained the organisation of a nineteenth-century 'little tea': 'A pretty little afternoon tea service is placed upon a small table and there are plates of rolled bread-and-butter, as well as biscuits and cake .... The hostess can either sit near the table or stand beside it whilst she pours the tea. If a gentleman happens to be present, it is his duty to hand the cups to the ladies; if not this office falls to the lot of the daughters of the house.' An alternative form of etiquette was 'to have tea made downstairs and kept going from four o'clock till half past five, the cups being brought up, poured out, by the parlour-maid or house-maid on a tray. This is quite correct, but perhaps less snug and sociable than the ordinary method.'

Offering cups of ready-poured tea meant that milk or cream was added to the tea. Victorian etiquette recognised this as the correct behaviour, yet in the early years of the twentieth century, William Ukers wrote that 'Milk or cream generally is added to the beverage in the cup. Cold milk is used by most people, but some prefer hot. It is placed in the cup before the tea is poured. In Scotland, where the cream is thin, it is used as a superior alternative to milk. In Western England, cream is not used much in tea as the milk is quite rich.' When it comes to the addition of milk, people from different classes and regions of Britain have always had different opinions. Cream or milk? Hot or cold? Poured into the empty cup or added to the tea? The debate is destined never to be resolved.

The boudoir at Lanhydrock in Cornwall. In this intimate, feminine sitting-room, Lady Robartes would entertain her friends to tea. The silver tea-service on the larger table dates from 1882–3, the silver-plated muffin dish from slightly earlier.

The Victorian servants' hall at Speke Hall on Merseyside, with the table laid as for high tea. The meal would typically have included soup, hot savoury dishes, puddings or cakes and plenty of strong tea.

HIGH TEA

In Mrs Beeton's 1892 edition of her *Book of Household Management*, she talks not only of 'afternoon tea' but also of 'high tea': 'in some old-fashioned places, whose inhabitants have not moved with the times ... a quiet tea where people are invited to partake of such nice things as hot buttered toast, tea cakes, new-laid eggs, and home-made preserves and cake'.

We do not know exactly when the first high tea was eaten. For the working and lower middle classes, it progressed naturally from the fact that tea was served as the standard beverage at mealtimes throughout the day. 'Dinner' still took place in the middle of the day. For men there was meat and vegetables, fish, or bread and cheese, depending on the family budget and the region. In the poorest homes, the women and children made do with tea. In Wales, as Marie Trevelyan wrote in 1893, 'the people dine at 12 or 12.30; they have tea at four o'clock, and supper about eight, when in some parts of Wales, the Curfew bell is still rung.'

For most poor families, however, there was rarely time for cups of tea in the middle of the afternoon. But a large pot of strong tea sitting in the middle of the meal table amidst cold meats, pies, fried bacon and potatoes, cheese, home-baked bread or oatmeal cakes was a welcome sight at 5.30 or 6pm at the end of the working day. A 'high tea' of filling, hearty foods, also known as 'meat tea' or 'great tea' was exactly what mine and factory workers needed as soon as they arrived home hungry and thirsty from a 10-hour shift.

Flora Thompson's *Lark Rise to Candleford* gives us all the details of a typical working-class evening tea: 'Here then were the three chief ingredients of the one hot meal a day, bacon from the flitch, vegetables from the garden, and flour for a roly-poly. This meal, called "tea", was taken in the evening, when the men were home from the fields and the children from school, for neither could get home at midday.' The meal varied from house to house and for tea at a nearby farm, 'there were fried ham and eggs, cakes and scones and stewed plums and cream, jam and jelly and junket'.

In Mrs Gaskell's novel, *Mary Barton*, set in Manchester, the preparations for an impromptu high tea are described: 'Then came a long whispering, and chinking of money ...' "Run, Mary dear, first round the corner, and get some fresh eggs at Tippings .... And see if he has any nice ham cut that he would let us have a pound of ... and Mary, you must get a pennyworth of milk and a loaf of bread – mind you get it fresh and new and – that's all, Mary." "No, it's not all," said her husband. "Thou must get sixpennyworth of rum to warm the tea ...".'

Even for the very poor, tea with bread provided the evening's nourishment. In 1853, the *Edinburgh Review* wrote: 'By her fireside, in her humble cottage, the lonely widow sits; the kettle simmers over the ruddy embers, and the blackened tea-pot on the hot brick prepares her evening drink. Her crust is scanty, yet as she sips the warm beverage – little sweetened, it may be, with the produce of the sugar-cane – genial thoughts awaken in her mind; her cottage grows less dark and lonely, and comfort seems to enliven the ill-furnished cabin.'

High tea in a country cottage, 'Living off the Fat of the Land': watercolour by Thomas Unwins (1782–1857). Hams, cheeses and home-baked bread feed the gathering . The farmer's wife tips more tea leaves into the pot, while the old lady beside her slurps tea from her saucer.

High tea was not exclusively a working-class meal. It was adopted by all social groups and adapted to their needs. The 1879 edition of Mrs Beeton's *Book of Household Management* explains:

There is Tea and Tea, the substantial family repast in the house of the early diner, and the afternoon cosy, chatty affairs that late diners have instituted…. The family tea-meal is very like that of breakfast, only that more cakes and knickknackery in the way of sweet eatables are provided. A 'High Tea' is where meat takes a prominent part, and signifies really what it is, a tea-dinner…. And there is the mere cup of tea that the lady or ladies of the house take after their afternoon drive as a kind of reviver before dressing for dinner. The afternoon tea signifies little more than tea and bread-and-butter, and a few elegant trifles in the way of cake and fruit. This meal is simply to enable a few friends to meet and talk comfortably and quietly….

Alice Christiana Smith's diary of her visit to the writer Thomas Hardy in August 1886 records, 'Back in time to dine with Eva, to Mr Hardy's where we had an old-fashioned cold supper tea'. Mrs Beeton told her readers that 'in some houses it is a permanent institution, quite taking the place of late dinner, and to many it is a most enjoyable meal, young people preferring it to dinner, it being a movable feast that can be partaken of at hours which will not interfere with tennis, boating or other amusements, and but little formality is needed.'

Families who employed servants very often took high tea on a Sunday in order to allow the maids and butler time to go to church and not worry about cooking an evening meal for the family. Nevertheless, there would be a grand array of sweet and savoury dishes to prepare. For high tea in a large country house, *Manners of Modern Society* recommended 'ripe red strawberries and jugs of rich cream … cakes of various kinds – plum, rice and sponge … hot muffins, crumpets, toast, tea-cakes…. The sideboard is the receptacle of the weightier matters, such as cold salmon, pigeon and veal and ham pies, boiled and roast fowls, tongues, ham, veal cake, and should it be a very "hungry tea", roast beef and lamb may be there for the gentlemen of the party.'

Today a 'cream tea' with scones and jam would probably include clotted cream. This was originally made in the south-west of England, where the rich pastures give milk the high fat content necessary. Here is a nineteenth-century recipe for 'Scald or Devonshire Cream'.

Take two gallons of new milk from the cow, strain it into a clean earthenware, put it into a cold place to remain undisturbed for 24 hours, then set it over a gentle clear charcoal fire until it is almost ready to boil, but let it not boyl for that will spoil all, then remove it to the place from whence it was taken and after twelve hours the Cream will be fit for use.

Note: If the Cream be left on the milk for 24 hours it will be the thicker and the butter made thereof will keep good, more than a week even in summer.

The dairy scullery at Lanhydrock, showing the scalding range where pans of milk were heated by hot-water pipes to make clotted cream.

A photograph from the 1880s showing the Prince and Princess of Wales being entertained to tea by the Rothschild family at Waddesdon Manor in Buckinghamshire. In the background, beyond the perilously angled tent, can be seen the fantastic towers of the Loire-style château.

ROYAL TEAS

Throughout her reign, Queen Victoria was a great tea drinker whose liking for the beverage and for afternoon tea made both even more popular. She was brought up at Kensington Palace, which the writer Leigh Hunt once said 'seems a place to drink tea in ... the reigns that flourished here ... were all tea-drinking reigns ... and if the present queen does not reign there, she was born and bred there'.

According to *The Private Life of the Queen* by 'one of Her Majesty's Servants', published in 1897,

Her Majesty has a strong weakness for afternoon tea. From her early days in Scotland, when [John] Brown and the other gillies used to boil the kettle in a sheltered corner of the moors while Her Majesty and the young Princesses sketched, the refreshing cup of tea has ever ranked high in the Royal favour. It is principally to supply the Queen's tea-table that the confectionery cooks are kept busy all the year round at Windsor, for wherever the Court may be there must follow a large supply of cakes.... The tea consumed in the palaces costs four shillings a pound, and the Queen drinks the same as every one else. Whether the Queen helps to boil the kettle herself, or whether it is brought to her ready made, she always loves her tea.

Tea brought comfort to the Queen and her household in troubled times. In March 1853, a fire had swept through part of Windsor Castle and the events of the following day were recorded in the letters of the Hon. Eleanor Stanley, one of her Maids of Honour:

The scene of wreck and ruin this morning was terrible, but they are making the outer rooms tidy as quick as they can.... I never saw anything so sweet as the Queen, for with all her composure one saw she was very anxious; and in the midst of it all, or rather, when it began to get a little better, she ordered tea to be brought for us, which I am sure none of us had thought of for ourselves; and looked quite pleased when the first person who took a cup was the Prince, who had the most awful cold, and came into the room just as the page brought in the tea-tray....

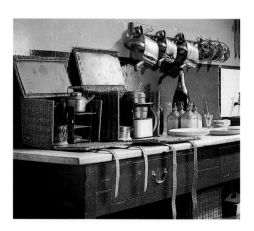

When the Queen was in Scotland tea played an important part in the day. In her diary for 1860, she recorded, 'We got up rather early, and sat working and reading in the drawing room till the breakfast was ready – good tea and bread and butter and some excellent porridge.' An entry for the previous year reads, 'We walked down to where we had lunched, and rode to the bottom. Here we found a fire, also tea with cakes etc., which had been very kindly prepared for us ... We drank the tea, and left in the carriage at half past six o'clock.'

In London, Queen Victoria introduced afternoon receptions at Buckingham Palace in 1865 and garden parties, known as 'breakfasts' in 1868. Over the years she also gave tea parties at Windsor for various groups. An event reported by *Woman's Weekly* on 30 December 1899 was typical, 'On Boxing Day, at St George's Hall, Windsor, Her Majesty with her customary solicitude and graciousness, entertained the wives and families of the Household Brigade, now at the front, as well as the wives of Reservists living in the Windsor district.' Everyone arrived at a quarter to four and, having greeted them, the Queen left while the guests sat down to tea. 'The Princesses were assiduous in their attentions to their guests, handing tea and offering cakes to all.'

AFTERNOON TEA.

Above: Queen Victoria was a great tea drinker, depicted with cup in hand by advertisers and, as here, in book illustrations.

Left: Detail of the butler's pantry at Cragside in Northumberland. The wicker hampers contain portable stoves for brewing up picnic teas during shooting parties on the grouse moors.

THE TEA-TIME MENU

In Victorian country houses, preparing recipes for tea was carried out not in the kitchens, but in the stillroom, where the maid was under the direct supervision of the housekeeper. The stillroom in previous centuries had been the province of the mistress of the house, where she prepared sweetmeats, confectionery and cordials for the banqueting or dessert course – providing yet another link between luxury food items and tea.

Afternoon tea, as Marie Bayard wrote in 1884 in *Hints on Etiquette*, was 'not supposed to be a substantial meal, merely a light refreshment'. The food and drink were then (and still are today) less important than the event itself. 'Cakes,' she said, 'thin bread and butter, and hot buttered scones, muffins, or toast are all the accompaniments strictly necessary.' *The Lady at Home and Abroad*, published in 1898, endorsed this view,

adding 'such things as champagne cup, foie gras sandwiches, macedoines of fruit, etc., would be considered outré and out of place'.

Neat, crustless sandwiches were a particularly useful tea-time food, allowing hostesses the possibility of introducing more exciting flavours. More important, perhaps, they could be eaten without risk of soiling gloves and other articles of clothing. Mrs Beeton told readers in 1892 that sandwiches 'intended for "afternoon tea" are dainty trifles, pleasing to the eye and palette, but too flimsy to allay hunger where it exists'. Whereas for some events the Victorians liked to decorate the outside of sandwiches 'with various coloured chaud-froid sauces', those intended for tea should be plain to protect the gloves.

Here are some recipes for biscuits, cakes, etc, that might have been served at a Victorian tea-table.

From a nineteenth-century recipe book at Dyrham Park

MILK DOUGH FOR CHILDREN'S CAKES

½ a stone of Currants to 1 stone flour, yeast & instead of water, mix with quite fresh warm milk. The quantity should be the same, as is generally used of the mix overnight. no Sugar.

TEA CAKES, BY MRS DAVIS, 1870–1

1 lb flour. 1 oz ½ butter melted into flour (1 Eggs into a tea cup full of milk) (Well beaten the Eggs + Milk) add a little salt & a teaspoonful of baking powder, put into a hot oven to take ¼ of an hour.

BREAD FOR TEA (MR BLYTHE)

To about 3lbs of flour, put 2ozs of butter melted in sufficient milk & make it into a stiff dough – Let it rise with a little yeast – When sufficiently risen make it up into dough, & add one egg. Make it into the shape desired. Egg over the top with a little yolk of egg. Bake in a moderately quick oven.

SEVILLE ORANGE BISCUITS

Peel whole Seville Oranges in two waters until tender, cut them and take out the pulp & juice – beat them in a Mortar and then pass them through a Sieve & put double the quantity of loaf Sugar beaten & sifted. When mixed, set them in the sun or before the fire to dry. When half dry cut them into what form you please. Keep in a dry place in a Box with layers of paper between them.

Mrs Bryer's recipe, Leamington, 1855

The stillroom at Tatton Park in Cheshire. Here the stillroom maid would prepare breakfasts and teas under the supervision of the housekeeper. Beyond the main table, laid with preparations for tea, is the brick baking oven with its iron door.

GINGER CAKE

½lb of loaf sugar moistened with a little water & powdered Jamaica ginger to your taste. 2 tablespoonsful of water & ½ teaspoonsful of ginger to the ½lb sugar, × ¼oz is rather too much for most people. Let it boil from 5 to 10 minutes, and pour it out into a shape placed on a slab till cold. Unless put in a shape it is apt to run too thin.

GINGERBREAD

1lb 2ozs of flour, the same of brown sugar, ¾ of a lb of butter, ½ a lb of treacle, 1oz & ¼ of ground ginger, 1 egg, the latter must be well rubbed in the flour, then mixed all together and rolled in round balls or cut in fingers, and baked in not too hot an oven.

Mr Blythe, July 9th 1858

BUTTERED EGGS (FOR HIGH TEA)

Take 5 or 6 eggs. beat them up in a Stew pan with 2ozs of butter, 3 tablespoonful of cream & the same of milk, some pepper & salt with a wooden spoon, put them on a slow fire and keep constantly drawing up the egg from the bottom as it bakes until all is done.

From Mary Ann Disraeli's nineteenth-century book of Receipts and Household Hints at Hughenden Manor, Buckinghamshire

SODA CAKE, MRS HEDLEY'S RECEIPT, DECEMBER 1845

½ lb currants ½lb loaf sugar ½lb butter 1lb flour ½ pint milk ¼ oz soda 3 eggs
The soda must dissolve in tepid Milk and all the other ingredients excepting the eggs which must be beaten to a light Froth and when the Milk etc is mixed with the flour and sufficiently cold to receive the Eggs then add them.

NB The butter must be rubbed in small pieces with the flour until it is quite smooth when all is worked together. Bake it in a moderately heated oven one hour and a quarter.

MACAROONS

Blanch 4oz of almonds and pound with 4 spoonsful of orange flower water whisk the whites of four eggs to a froth then mix it to a pound of sugar sifted with the almonds to a paste, lay a sheet of wafer paper on a tin and put it on in little cakes the shape of macaroons.

SPUNGE CAKE

16 eggs and half the whites beat into a thick froth a pound of sugar pounded small a pint of the best flower, when beat with a spoon for an hour will be light then add a glass of brandy, bake in a moderately warm Oven.

CHEAP BREAD

Boil half a pound rice in two quarts of water 40 or 50 minutes and mix it with a peck of flour. The bread will not be injured in quality, though increased in quantity about a third.

Detail of the fireplace in the housekeeper's room at Uppark in Sussex. A clever system of trivets attached to the bars of the coal grate enabled the housekeeper and her maid to boil up tea and coffee and keep them hot.

A formal afternoon dress with train bought in 1889. The matching bodice and skirt are of black figured silk patterned with a willow-leaf design.

TEA GOWNS

What to wear for tea was an important question preoccupying both guests and hostesses. Marie Bayard advised 'it is fashionable, but not in the least necessary, for the hostess to wear a tea-gown ... should she not care to adopt this style of toilette, any nice afternoon dress will do. It is not necessary to wear gloves, but when there are a large number to receive, it is pleasanter for the hostess to do so especially if she has at all warm hands.' If ladies did choose to wear gloves, they were 'not removed when tea only is taken, but occasionally it is necessary to take them off'. At afternoon dances, 'ladies retain their hats and bonnets'.

Tea gowns evolved in the 1870s, at a time when afternoon tea had been established as an eminently feminine and indulgent time of the day. *Beauty & Fashion* summed this up in its edition of 6 December 1890:

The first important item with a hostess in regard to afternoon tea is the selection of a becoming gown. The tea will taste sweeter, and the cups will look prettier, if she is robed in some gauze-like fabric of artistic make, and a dainty tea-gown is of just as much consequence to her as the beverage itself, and adds considerably to her good humour. If she knows that she is well-clad, and that the pretty, flimsy lace and soft silk will bear the closest inspection of her particular friends, there is sure to be a charming air of satisfaction pervading her whole conversation, and her manner will be more than usually affable and gracious.

A debate was raging in the letter pages of fashion magazines as to the dangers or otherwise of tight lacing. Corsets were absolutely necessary to those who wished to achieve the desired 18-inch waist (and some ladies even aimed at 14 or 15 inches), but caused all manner of medical problems. Many spoke out against the dangers of such garments, even comparing the fashion for tight lacing to the Chinese practice of binding women's feet, or the insertion of a piece of stone into the lower lip of some African women. In 1884, an International Health Exhibition in Kensington included a section on dress and laid emphasis on the need to move away from the distorting and constricting use of boned corsets.

In keeping with this trend, afternoon tea gowns were designed to allow the female body a freedom that more formal Victorian dress did not. Soft flowing folds of cashmere, cotton, chiffon, ninon and lace were decorated with ribbons and pearls, crystals and velvet, bows and braiding to create fantasy gowns in which ladies draped themselves delicately on sofas with a porcelain cup and saucer in one hand. And, although these gowns were almost certainly worn over corsets by those who felt that their natural shape needed a little help, they could also be worn without and yet allow the wearer to feel and look extremely elegant and feminine. The flowing shape and soft fabrics suited the relative informality of tea with friends in the boudoir or garden, although they were not intended to be worn when going out to tea.

For some, it was also acceptable for dinner or evening wear at home, as an article in the *Princess* in November 1890 explained: 'The tea gown is a garment that has undergone many changes; it was at first a wrap intended for the use of those ladies who take their tea in luxurious privacy, but speedily advanced from semi-seclusion, and was admitted at the quiet dinner or as an evening gown. Now it is to all intents and purposes a reception toilette for the afternoon.'

By the 1890s, all the top fashion houses of London and Paris were offering an elaborate range of tea gowns. *Beauty & Fashion*, on 17 January 1891, reviewed the week's latest fashions: 'There is an increasing demand for pretty evening dresses and tea gowns and we believe there has never been such a varied assortment for ladies to choose from.'

Liberty tea gown bought by Alice, Marchioness of Bristol, in 1897. The bodice is of green satin, with outer sleeves, yoke and girdle in moss-green velvet embroidered with flowers of topaz and beads. The puffed inner sleeves, neck ruching and hem are sky-green chiffon.

CHILDREN'S TEAS

In wealthy Victorian homes the children lived at the top of the house, sometimes behind a green baize door to allow the rest of the household a certain amount of peace and quiet. They grew up under the watchful eye of nannies, nurses and governesses who shared the nursery floor with their charges and oversaw their daily routine, including mealtimes. Tea – usually a combined high tea/supper – was as much a part of this routine as afternoon tea was for adults. At four or five o'clock, books and toys were put away, hands were washed and high chairs pulled up to the table for a combined tea meal of sardine sandwiches, boiled eggs with fingers of bread and butter (often called soldiers or soldier boys), banana sandwiches, muffins and crumpets, scones, gingerbread, fruitcake, chocolate cake and biscuits.

As a Victorian governess, Anne Bronte's eponymous heroine, Agnes Grey, had to deal with the precocious behaviour of her spoilt charges. 'I had all my meals in the schoolroom with my pupils at such times as suited their fancy: sometimes they would have tea at four; frequently they would storm at the servants because it was not in precisely at five.' Similarly, Georgiana Sitwell recalled that 'as young children [in the 1830s] ...

our tea was at six, after which we went to sit at our parents' dinner table during dessert, between seven and eight o'clock.'

If the children were old enough to go to school, they would have 'nursery tea' as soon as they got home. Even if the family was away from home, tea was still an everyday event. Georgiana Sitwell remembered that while travelling as a child, she and her siblings on one occasion were obliged to sleep at a hotel and 'How delighted were we with its comfort! The bedrooms were very small but exquisitely clean, the beds excellent, and oh! What muffins at our unusually sumptuous schoolroom tea.'

If she was not busy with visitors or household concerns, the children's mother sometimes joined the group in the nursery for a cup of tea. But generally children did not spend very much time with their parents, only going downstairs after 'tea' for an hour or so to walk with their mama in the garden, to look at books, or to talk or play.

Tea-parties were regarded as special events. In 1860, the headmaster of the Quaker school at Ackworth in Yorkshire was forced to take some time off work because of ill health. On his return, he found that the pupils had been so well behaved during his absence that he rewarded them with an evening tea-party. All the cups and saucers were borrowed

from the village and the entire school sat down together for its first proper traditional English tea. It was a huge success and was remembered 'for those who had the pleasure in participating in it as one of the most delightful occasions of their school-days'.

Victorian birthday and Christmas celebrations often included tea-parties for the children and their friends, with a feast of special treats to eat, a big birthday cake with candles to blow out, fancy dress, games to play, sometimes a visiting conjuror or magician, ventriloquist or magic lantern show, and, before they went home, gifts for all the guests. Books of etiquette recommended that refreshments at a 'juvenile party should be simple in character, but an abundance of bon-bons is a sine qua non'.

The nursery at Berrington Hall in Herefordshire, with a dolls' tea at the small table in the foreground, and a nursery tea of boiled eggs laid on the main table. Hot buttered toast or muffins would have been kept warm in the copper muffin dish.

Tea-party for willow workers, Somerset, c.1900.

TEA FOR THE WORKERS

For many poor Victorian families, a hard day's work had to be carried out on a less than full stomach. Young men were often sent off in the morning after a meagre breakfast of potatoes and tea to walk several miles to their place of work. Lunch was dry bread with perhaps a little cheese in good times, and more potatoes and tea at home in the evening.

During the working day, farm workers and labourers generally drank beer, but in 1878, T. Bland Garland, a landowner with somewhat revolutionary ideas, wrote that 'nothing could be more unsuitable to quench the thirst during hard work in hot weather than beer'. He resolved not to supply any more beer but agreed to pay the men 18 shillings instead of 14, and the women 9 shillings instead of 7. And because he recognised that they would still have to quench their thirst somehow and would probably end up in the public house, he decided to supply them with a limitless amount of tea. He purchased a flat-bottomed 8½-gallon boiler, took it out to the fields in a cart, built a temporary fireplace from bricks and organised for a local woman to light the fire each morning, boil the water, boil up the tea, add milk and sugar to it ready for the workmen to 'take as much as they like at all times of the day, beginning at breakfast time, and ending when they leave off work at night'. He advised other farmers to do the same but to ensure that the tea 'be good and made with care in the field, not sent out from the house, or there will not be enough; be sure that it is always within reach of every labourer, without stint'. What a wise and sensible man!

Those who followed his lead found that their men worked much better – not really surprising if one considers how much beer would have been swilled during a working day and the evening that followed. Sir Philip Rose noticed that his farm workers 'were in better condition at the conclusion of the day, less stupid and sullen, and certainly much better fitted the next morning to resume their labours, than with the old system of beer'.

On the farms around Lark Rise, Flora Thompson described how, 'At twelve by the sun, the teams would knock off for the dinner-hour ... and men and boys threw themselves down on sacks ... and tin bottles of cold tea were uncorked and red handkerchiefs of food unwrapped ... .' All around the country, workers refreshed themselves with hot or cold tea – in factories, mines, offices and farmers' fields, on railways, roads and fishing boats. Tea had become the best drink of the day.

Tea can used by farmworkers to carry tea out to the fields.

In the workhouses, home to the penniless in society who had nowhere else to go, the provision of tea was one of the major concerns of the committees running them. At one such institution in Aberystwyth in Wales, the daily diet consisted of bread, potatoes, gruel, a little cooked meat, soup and rice or suet puddings. In addition, 'The old people of sixty years of age and upwards may be allowed 1 oz tea and 7 oz sugar in addition per week'. The women under 60 were allowed half a pint of tea for breakfast, but in 1869 this was increased to one pint.

Southwell Workhouse in Nottinghamshire made similar provision. From its inception in 1824, the diet of most inmates consisted of breakfast and dinner of bread and milk or milk-porridge, a more substantial midday meal but no tea. However, notes kept by the founder, Rev. Beecher, say, 'The aged, infirm and guiltless Poor, are not strictly subjected to the ordinary Diet; but are allowed Tea, a small quantity of Butter, and other little indulgences of this description.' The workhouse account book shows that two tin tea kettles were purchased for Southwell in 1824 for 2s 9d and 1s 6d. When the workhouse was taken into the national system, similar provision was made: 'old people of 60

The early nineteenth-century workhouse just outside Southwell in Nottinghamshire. In the centre are the master's quarters, with the committee room on the first floor, where representatives from rural parishes would meet up to discuss the running of the workhouse, fortified by meals and beverages. The inmates were strictly segregated, with compartments for men, women and children, the idle and the profligate, the blameless and the infirm. Only the aged, infirm and guiltless poor might be provided with tea as part of their diet.

years upwards may be allowed one ounce of tea, five ounces of butter and seven ounces of sugar per week'. By 1841, tea was still considered a treat for special occasions such as Christmas when inmates were given 'plum pudding and roast beef ... for Dinner and Cake and Tea for Supper'.

Tea has a strong link with work-houses through Louisa Twining from the long-established family of tea merchants. She founded the Workhouse Visiting Society in 1859, campaigning to raise standards in workhouse infirmaries and to achieve improved care for the children.

Sir Hubert von Herkomer's moving portrait of old ladies in the workhouse, Eventide: A Scene in the Westminster Union, *painted in 1878. Herkomer, particularly noted for his social genre works, has imbued the ladies with dignity, despite the shabbiness of their surroundings.*

As in the eighteenth century, tea was recognised as such an important part of everybody's life that employers were expected to calculate a certain amount of their servants' monthly wages to be paid in tea. *The Cook's Oracle* by Dr William Kitchiner, published in 1823, calculated half a pound of tea at £3 10s per month per annum, and the same amount of sugar per week as the average for a female servant. Other items allowed for were four pairs of shoes, two pairs of black worsted stockings, two pairs of white cotton stockings, two gowns, six aprons, a bonnet, a shawl, a cloak and various ribbons, handkerchiefs, threads, needles, scissors and other working tools.

A document from the household papers at Erddig records that the total consumption of 'servants' tea' in 1848 was '54lb @ 3s 4d per lb, and 45lbs of coffee @ 1s 10d.' Mrs Beeton's 1861 edition of her *Book of Household Management* recommended the following amounts for domestic servants:

WAGES	WHEN NO EXTRA ALLOWANCE IS MADE FOR TEA, SUGAR & BEER	WHEN AN EXTRA ALLOWANCE IS MADE FOR TEA, SUGAR & BEER
The Housekeeper	*From £20 to £45*	*From £18 to £40*
The Lady's Maid	*From £12 to £25*	*From £10 to £20*
The Head Nurse	*From £15 to £30*	*From £13 to £26*
The Cook	*From £14 to £30*	*From £12 to £26*
The Upper Housemaid	*From £12 to £20*	*From £10 to £17*

Young housewives relied on the advice of writers like Mrs Beeton to make sure that they treated servants correctly.

Some employers, perhaps with socialist leanings, believed that there should be more kindness and contact between employer and employee. Towards the end of the century, some aristocratic families started organising regular tea-parties for their staff in the family reception or drawing room. Tea was seen as the great leveller that allowed people from different social classes to mingle without too many awkward moments. But in *The Admirable Crichton*, J.M. Barrie captured the attitude of those who thought the entire exercise ridiculous and embarrassing for all concerned. Crichton was the long-suffering butler with sincere doubts.

The Admirable Crichton [ACT

but the daughters of the house cannot tell you of whom; 'there is a catalogue somewhere.' There are a thousand or so of roses in basins, several library novels, and a row of weekly illustrated newspapers lying against each other like fallen soldiers. If any one disturbs this row Crichton seems to know of it from afar and appears noiselessly and replaces the wanderer. One thing unexpected in such a room is a great array of tea things. Ernest spots them with a twinkle and has his epigram at once unsheathed. He dallies, however, before delivering the thrust.

ERNEST

I perceive, from the tea cups, Crichton, that the great function is to take place here.

CRICHTON

(*With a respectful sigh*) Yes, sir.

ERNEST

(*Chuckling heartlessly*) The servants' hall coming up to have tea in the drawing-room. (*With terrible sarcasm*) No wonder you look happy, Crichton.

CRICHTON.

(*Under the knife*) No, sir.

ERNEST

Do you know, Crichton, I think that with an effort you might look even happier. (CRICHTON *smiles wanly.*) You don't approve of his lordship's compelling his servants to be his equals —once a month?

CRICHTON

It is not for me, sir, to disapprove of his lordship's Radical views.

ERNEST

Certainly not. And, after all, it is only once a month that he is affable to you.

CRICHTON

On all other days of the month, sir, his lordship's treatment of us is everything that could be desired.

ERNEST

(*This is the epigram*) Tea cups! Life, Crichton, is like a cup of tea; the more heartily we drink, the sooner we reach the dregs.

CRICHTON

(*Obediently*) Thank you, sir.

Whereas servants no doubt hated such gatherings, they could enjoy their own tea-parties below stairs. A footman by the name of Thomas who worked for the Dukes of Sutherland at Trentham Hall in Staffordshire and at their house in London, recalled in his diary how he was often invited to tea in the stillroom. He would return the favour by inviting the stillroom maids and the kitchen maids to tea in his pantry. It is important to remember that on each level of a prosperous household, tea played a significant part in everybody's life, from the nursery on the top floor to the servants' hall in the basement.

Above: High Life Below Stairs, *servants and one of their guests enjoying tea from a painting by Charles Hunt (1829–1900). Although not as sophisticated as afternoon tea in the drawing room upstairs, this pause in the working day was no less important.*

These monthly gatherings

LORD LOAM

(*Shaking hands with his valet*) How do you do, Rolleston?

Left: Excerpt from the first act of J.M.Barrie's The Admirable Crichton, *published in 1914, in which the butler views with gloom the forthcoming tea-party where the family will mingle with their servants. The cartoon by Hugh Thomson reflects the stiffness of the occasion.*

TEA, TEMPERANCE AND HEALTH

For centuries alcohol had been part of the daily diet in Britain, with ale or beer featuring at all mealtimes and cele-brations. Birthdays, anniversaries, weddings, christening, funerals, the completion of apprenticeship, the starting of a new job, coming of age, the achieving of qualifications – all involved the consumption of copious amounts of alcohol. Drinking and being drunk were accepted as normal behaviour and those who refused to join in were ridiculed and ostracised. At the beginning of the nineteenth century, such drunken and bawdy behaviour amongst the majority of the population, the sight of mothers, their tiny babies in their arms, falling over in the street in a drunken stupor, and a recognition of the evils and dangers associated with alcohol, prompted the beginning of the Temperance Movement. The movement started in the 1820s in Scotland and Ireland, possibly because consumption of alcohol was markedly

higher there. Within two or three years, it had spread to England and Wales. A Welsh minister, the Rev. R. Thomas, wrote that 'The alarming increase of drunkenness made thinking people shudder, the frequent lapses of professing Christians through strong drink was a source of constant trouble to the churches of the various denominations.'

Members of the early temperance societies took a pledge only against spirits such as whisky, gin and rum, but still allowed beer and wine, believing that total abstinence would be too harsh for most people. But teetotalism was the inevitable next step. In 1831, English merchant ships started sailing without any alcohol on board, and the government made allowances for tea, sugar and coffee to be taken on board duty free for voyages that would last more than 40 days. The following year, Richard Turner, a working man from Preston in Lancashire, made a speech advocating total abstinence from alcohol. Where the Preston movement led, the temperance societies followed, urging

people to drink tea instead. It is unclear whether the term teetotal resulted as a link between tea and temperance, but the first appearance of the word coincided with those early fund-raising, alcohol-free tea-parties.

In *Tea and Tea Drinking*, Arthur Reade described a tea-party of the Preston Temperance Society, held at Christmas in 1833 and attended by about 1,200 people.

At the upper and lower ends of each side-room were mottoes in large characters, 'temperance, sobriety, peace, plenty', and in the centre of the room a-connecting the others was displayed in similar characters, the motto 'happiness'. The tables were divided and numbered, and eighty sets of brilliant tea-requisites, to accommodate parties of ten persons each, were placed on the table with two candles for each party. A boiler capable of containing 200 gallons was set up .... About forty men, principally reformed drunkards, were busily engaged as waiters, water-carriers, etc; those who waited at table wore white aprons with 'temperance' printed on the front.

THE STAMFORD MERCURY WROTE ON 22 MAY 1840,

Last week, the bricklayers in the employ of Wm. Bennett, Esq., Mayor of Grimsby, had their mould washing, which in former years was a drunken and disorderly carouse of strong beer, occasioning to many two or three day's loss of time, and ending in quarrels and bloodshed: but this time their employer gave them flour, and all partook of plum-cake and tea; the evening was spent in joy and harmony, and in social conversation instead of quarrelling; and of those who were not already teetotallers, fifteen signed the pledge … .

Sir Walter Calverley Trevelyan of Wallington in Northumberland was known as the Apostle of Temperance. As an ardent teetotaller and President of the United Kingdom Alliance, he campaigned for the total abolition of all alcohol. When he inherited his father's home at Nettlecombe Court in Somerset, he emptied most of the contents of the wine cellar into the lake. At Wallington he kept the cellars firmly locked and licences for liquor on the estate were abolished. Sir Walter's will bequeathed all wines and spirits in the Wallington and Nettlecombe cellars to Dr Benjamin Ward Richardson for scientific purposes. In compliance with the wishes of the Trevelyan family, the estate at Wallington, including the village of Cambo, is still 'dry' and tea offers an excellent alternative for the National Trust staff who work there.

As the Temperance Movement developed, so the number of recruits grew rapidly. William Carter described a number of 'extraordinary tea meetings' in his book, *The Power of Truth*, written in 1865: 'Upwards of seventy teas have been given to different companies since my book, *The Power of God*, was published. The average number of each meeting was from four to five hundred so that upwards of 30,000 have been brought under the sound of the gospel.' Making tea for such huge numbers presented problems for the organisers but ingenuity helped them devise new ways of coping. At a meeting in Birmingham, 'they made the tea in large tins, about a yard square, and a foot deep, each one containing as much as will serve about 250 persons.

Temperance poster from 1850, announcing a tea festival hard on the heels of Christmas. Newspaper reports describe how the people who attended often 'had scarcely anywhere to go, met together with kind friends in this way, and had a pleasant night, a friendly cup of tea and felt all the better for it when they went away'.

The tea is tied loosely in bags, about ¼ lb in each. At the top there is an aperture, into which the boiling water is conveyed by a pipe from the boiler, and at one corner there is a tap, from which the tea, when brewed, is drawn out. It may be either sweetened, or milked, or both ... capital tea was made at the last festival by this plan.'

Tea-meetings proved so successful that other organisations started holding them as well. The Anti-Corn Law League, fighting to reduce the price of bread by allowing the free importation of foreign grain, held tea-meetings in the 1840s to attract attention to their cause. The Vegetarian Society followed suit with high teas of salad, fruit and home-baked bread served with tea, coffee and cocoa.

Tea now provided a focus for healthier living, an alternative to the alcohol that had for centuries ruined the health and lives of millions. In *Some Observations on the Medicinal and Dietic Properties of Green Tea* in 1827, W. Newnham wrote that

green tea is found to be particularly useful in the headache produced by the stimulation of alcoholic fluids: and in a similar affection arising from intense and long-continued application of the mind to any particular object of literary research: and there are few who have

not experienced its salutary influence under such circumstances, in soothing the irritation – calming the nervous system – invigorating the animal frame – refreshing the jaded spirits – clearing the ideas – brightening the faculties – and so far recruiting the energies of the brain, as to render it again a willing and obedient organ.

Mrs Beeton, in 1861, reported the views of 'our great nurse', Florence Nightingale. She felt that too much tea could be a bad thing for invalids, but that a little could be beneficial:

A great deal too much against tea is said by wise people, and a great deal too much of it is given to the sick by foolish people. When they see the natural and almost universal craving in English sick for their tea, you cannot but feel that nature knows what she is about. But a little tea or coffee restores them quite as much as a great deal; and a great deal of tea, and especially of coffee, impairs the little power of digestion they have; yet a nurse, because she sees how one or two cups of tea or coffee restore her patient, thinks three or four cups will do twice as much. This is not the case at all: it is however, certain that there is nothing yet discovered which is a substitute to the English patient for his cup of tea.

OUT TO TEA

From the 1840s, following closely in the wake of the Temperance Movement came temperance restaurants and hotels, coffee houses, refreshment houses and tea rooms. Their aim was to offer cheap food and non-alcoholic beverages in surroundings that appealed to the less well-off, thereby encouraging them away from public houses, inns and taverns. At first, the majority of these new catering outlets seem to have been cafés, coffee houses or coffee taverns, but they all served a range of beverages, including tea. During 1878, *The Caterer and Refreshment Contractors' Gazette* ran a series of articles with such titles as 'How to Establish a Coffee-House', 'The Cheap Coffee House Movement', 'Coffee-House Fitting and Decoration', and 'Coffee Houses in Cheap Neighbourhoods'. In October of the same year, it calculated that there were 1,309 coffee taverns in England and 57 in Wales. The journal also offered advice on how to brew and serve tea and coffee, warning readers, 'Inferior tea is not economical in use … . The proportions may be three quarters of a pound of tea to seventeen pints of water, with three quarters of a pound of sugar. A small quantity of milk – two or three teaspoonfuls – may be added to each cup when served.'

In the 1880s, the vogue for cheap coffee houses gave way to a new fashion for tea houses. The exact date is not known, but some time in 1884, the Aerated Bread Company (ABC), a chain of bakery shops, opened its first tea room and started a trend that was to be followed by other bakery companies, and by dairies, tobacco companies, chocolate manufacturers and ladies' clubs. The story goes that it was the enterprising manageress of the ABC's London Bridge branch who had the idea of turning a spare back room into a public tea room. Her plan worked so well that the company opened similar tea rooms and restaurants all over London. In 1889, an ABC prospectus for new branches around the country said, 'The Aerated Bread Company Limited of London have opened between fifty and sixty shops … in the City and West End … and they are frequented to an enormous extent by persons of both sexes: the main features … being cleanliness and purity, combined with comfort and cheapness.'

The *South Wales Daily News* wrote of the ABC in April 1889, 'The London Company was, in its original form, a bread dealing company solely; latterly it has extended its business to supplying tea, coffee, etc. with first class cakes and pastry, which have given it a commanding position in the lighter refreshment business.' But this prime position was soon to be challenged by other catering establishments.

By 1893, Lockharts had 50 coffee rooms in London and Liverpool. Next came the Express Dairy, and then Kardomah, a tea and coffee business with shops in Paris as well as around Britain. Perhaps the most important name to emerge from this period was Joseph Lyons. Founded in 1886, and developing out of a family tobacco firm, Joseph Lyons moved into catering by running refreshment stalls at trade exhibitions: his first big contract was at the Barnum & Bailey Show at London's Olympia. The first Lyons tea room was opened in 1894 at 213 Piccadilly. By December 1895, Lyons had opened fourteen more tea rooms which prompted *The Caterer and Hotelkeeper's Gazette* to remark, 'In view of the rocket-like rise of Mssrs J. Lyons & Co. (Limited) as entertainment and refreshment caterers, who shall say that the field of remunerative enterprise in our particular line is already exhausted?'

An anonymous report in Lyons' archives explained the success of their tea rooms:

Hitherto, there had been nowhere for Mama and the children to have a cup of tea or a midday meal. Prices too had been extortionate. In short, Lyons introduced to Londoners, and later to the provinces, good cheap food with exceptional smartness and cleanliness: it also gave fresh dignity to the occupation of catering. The new white and gold tea shops with their uniformed and attractive waitresses, shone forth in a London drab with drinking dens, dingy coffee houses and 'Slap Bangs' which were staffed by slipshod waiters and unkempt girls serving beer, coffee or tea.

While large companies were gaining fame with their chains of shops, many smaller enterprises were also being established. These announcements of teashops are from the Caterer & Hotel Proprietors' Gazette *for 10 July 1894. Between 1884 and 1900, the pages of the gazette were full of notices for similar establishments all over the country.*

MR. GEORGE WARD, late warrant officer in the Royal Warwickshire Regiment, has gone into the Bowling Green Hotel, Warwick, up to recently in the hands of Mr. F. Bennett.

MR. MYERS, formerly of Church Street, York, has recently become proprietor of a small hotel in Tanner Row, York, called The Grapes. It used to be a popular hostelry in the days of the old York Station.

THE BURLINGTON TEA ROOMS are now open, nearly opposite Burlington House, Piccadilly. The saloon is commodious, airy, and neatly equipped, mirrors and pictures being plentiful on the walls. As the tariff is quite moderate and the viands of good quality, the place should not want customers.

MRS. HICKIN, the widow of Mr. W. R. Hickin, formerly manager of the Woolacombe Bay Hotel, North Devon, has taken a temperance hotel there, and converted it into the Avondale House Boarding Establishment. It is capitally situated near the sea, and will, we trust, prove a success in Mrs. Hickin's hands.

A CHARMING innovation has been introduced at the fashionable lounge of the " Ladies Own " Tea Association in Bond Street. The lounge has been turned into an indoor garden. The walls are covered with green trellis work, the floor with green felt, there is a fountain, a rockery occupies the fireplace, and there are rustic seats and gates amidst flowering plants and spreading palms. This Association was originally founded by Miss Lambert and Miss Bartlett, who started an agency to dispose of Ceylon teas. Then five more friends brought in capital, and the concern was registered as a limited company, when the Bond Street Tea Rooms were opened. The Association now has over 150 lady agents in various parts of the country. The " town garden " idea is novel, and seems to be very popular.

Of all the main cities away from London, Glasgow gained a special reputation as a centre for excellent quality, reasonably priced tea rooms. In 1903, *The Builder's Journal and Architectural Record* reported: 'Glasgow is a very Tokio for tea-rooms. Nowhere can one have so much for so little, and nowhere are such places more popular or frequented.' The main characters in the important part played by Glasgow at this time were the Cranstons. In the 1870s, Stuart Cranston, son of a successful Glasgow hotelier, and an enterprising and energetic tea retailer, introduced the innovative idea of offering free samples of his various teas for customers to taste. This led him to provide tables and chairs for the clients' comfort, and he charged two pence for a cup of tea with sugar and cream (bread and cakes cost a little extra). And so Britain's first tea room opened in 1875 at 2 Queen Street. Three years later, Cranston's younger sister Kate decided to start her own business and opened the Crown Tea Rooms in Argyle Street. Success was immediate, and she went on to open two more tea rooms in 1886 and 1897 before commissioning Charles Rennie Mackintosh to design the interior of her next venture, the Willow Tea Rooms in Sauchiehall Street in the heart of town in 1903 (see page 164).

The most important feature of all these tea rooms and teashops was the appeal they had for people from all walks of life. The tea was excellent, the food was cheap, and the venues themselves ideal for lunchtime breaks, afternoon chats, relaxing moments away from the office or the house. Customers appreciated the hint of elegance that a visit to a teashop added to their otherwise humdrum days. Most important of all, tea rooms provided a safe place for women of all types and ages to relax over a little refreshment. In the 1880s, the Holborn Restaurant in London offered quiet, attention and comfort for 'ladies attending exhibitions or out shopping'. Men had always been able to go off to their clubs or to dine out in restaurants, hotels or public dining rooms. Ladies could certainly eat out if they were with their husbands or fathers, but what were they to do during the day when they were in need of something to eat or drink? There really was nowhere for a respectable lady to go. Now teashops provided the answer and it has even been suggested that their existence helped the progress of the movement for women's suffrage in Britain by creating a forum where women could talk freely and exchange views.

The British public now expected to be able to buy a decent cup of tea almost anywhere. In June 1896 *The Caterer and Hotelkeeper's Gazette* reported that the London County Council, on the recommendations of the Parks Committee, had sanctioned the following alterations: 'Hot water to be supplied separately to visitors at 1d per quart; ½d to be charged for each person using a chair, teapot, tea cup, saucer, etc., without refreshments; and 1d for a half-pint cup of tea, and 2d per fresh made pot of three gills and 3d per pint pot.'

The mural created by Charles Rennie Mackintosh in 1897 for the lunch gallery at Miss Cranston's tea rooms in Buchanan Street, Glasgow. The Bailie wrote of it: 'Elegant as the new establishment is as seen from the street, its interior is no less elegant, the decorations being in excellent taste, and showing to much effect.'

Engraving from the Graphic, *1892, showing
afternoon tea at a lawn tennis tournament;
'although lawn tennis has grown increasingly
popular, the tea perhaps, especially in the
country, plays a more important part in the
afternoon's programme'.*

Out in the streets, there were stalls selling tea and coffee day and night. The quality of the drinks and food offered was poor and would not have attracted any but poorer working folk, but at least they could get some refreshment at the start or end of their working day. In 1877, John Diprose wrote in *London Life*, 'a cup of hot coffee at the modest charge of one penny ... the dark brown muddy fluid, that bears no other affinity to the decoction you asked for ... equally suspicious tea is also to be had here, and for the masticatory delights, slices of bread plastered with strong-smelling butter or grease, and dark, dusty segments of stony plum cake.'

The tea room and tea terrace of the Houses of Parliament are still vital locations for politicians to gather for discussion and general political conversation. In July 1896, a new caterer was brought in to manage the tea facilities at Westminster. Mrs Moss proved a big financial success, with her strawberries, ice, tea, cream and biscuits yielding a return of over £25 per week. *The Caterer and Hotelkeeper's Gazette* recorded the universal approval, especially from the temperance members 'who hold that it is better for a law-giver to take tea in the open air, than whisky under cover. Tea on the Terrace is, as a daily contemporary puts it, a politician's "higher education".'

Cycling was all the rage. In June 1896, the Ladies' Own Tea Association of Bond Street opened a depot in Hyde Park, which was much frequented by fashionable cyclists. Cycles, charabancs and trains also conveyed families out into the countryside for a day away from the dirt and grime and noise of the cities. Of course, picnic teas were part of the fun for all classes and ages. The 23 May 1891 edition of *Beauty & Fashion* described typical summer scenes: 'We often see parties of merrymakers at picnics, or up the river, taking their tennis net, rackets, and balls with them for the whole paraphernalia is not much trouble to carry, and they can pitch the net at some suitable spot and enjoy a good game, whilst their companions of a more sedate order prepare the tea things and boil the

kettle.' For those who had not brought their own tea with them on the back of a bicycle or pony and trap, a little country tea room or tea garden would provide a refreshing pot of tea and some tea-time treats to restore the energy needed to make the journey back to town.

By the 1890s, tourism was becoming the great leisure activity in Britain. Photographs of Stonehenge, the nation's most famous ancient monument, showed visitors arriving en masse by bicycle, charabanc and carriage to view the stones. Punch speculated about how the site might be popularised by various activities, including tea and shrimps, in a cartoon in 1897.

HOW STONEHENGE MIGHT BE POPULARISED IF THE GOVERNMENT BOUGHT IT. SUGGESTION GRATIS.

Advertisement from the 15 February 1884 edition of the Caterer & Hotel Proprietors' Gazette *declaring the merits of the 'Special' block tin urn for tea, coffee or cocoa.*

TEA WARES

As tea prices came down, the size of teapots increased and so, as a result, did that of kettles. These became so unwieldy and heavy that ladies could no longer easily manage elegantly to pour the boiling water into their porcelain and silver teapots. The tea urn had thus become a fashionable and decorative alternative, gracing many Victorian tea-tables. At Dyrham Park, an inventory from 1839 lists a bronze tea urn with tea trays and a copper kettle kept in the butler's pantry. By 1871, the urn was listed in the inner pantry with a bronze tea kettle and four tea trays.

The nineteenth century was a time of great innovation and invention, and the creation and design of the perfect teapot was a challenge taken up by many. The basic shape remained relatively constant, altering slightly with the changes in design fashion. Details varied according to the inventiveness of the manufacturer. The Cadogan pot was filled from below; the Castleford had a sliding brass lid. Pots with two chambers and a filter between were designed on Chinese lines. Self-pouring pots with a pump action allowed ladies to pour without lifting the pot from the table. Other new ideas also caught the attention of the press. In May 1896, *The Caterer and Hotelkeeper's Gazette* announced the invention of a tea infuser (very familiar to us today) called a 'Teaette': 'It consists of a deep spoon bowl, perforated with small holes and slits, and having attached to it by hinges a duplicate spoon-bowl .... The idea is that the spoon should be filled with the requisite amount of tea, then be plunged into a cup or pot full of boiling water, and withdrawn after a few minutes infusion. The "Teaette" should be most useful for travelling luncheon-baskets, and might be introduced by caterers in tea-rooms ....'

European potteries and porcelain manufacturers started making full tea and breakfast sets in the 1790s, but until the second half of the nineteenth century, they were generally found only in the homes of wealthier families. The earliest sets consisted of twelve tea bowls, twelve straight-sided coffee cups, twelve saucers, a slop bowl, a sugar bowl, sometimes with its own lid, a milk jug, plates for bread and butter and two teapots. Smaller side plates were not introduced until the mid-nineteenth century, when they were needed for the regular service of sand-wiches and pastries at afternoon tea.

The better off owned at least one tea-service and grand houses owned several. The 1871 inventory for Dyrham Park listed 'part of a pink and white Tea Service, Best China Tea Service, Blue and Gold Border; twenty three Tea Cups and Saucers, Two Bread and Butter Plates; part of a Tea Service, Drab and Gold border; part of a Tea Service Sprig Pattern; Part of a White Tea Service; Part of Breakfast and Tea Service with Pink Border'. At Tatton Park in Cheshire, the plethora of tea-services owned by the Egerton family can be seen in the China Closet, where they are displayed along with a 900-piece glass service stored in wooden coffers.

A stereoscopic photograph showing a Victorian family tea, with the maidservant carrying the kettle. According to Isabella Beeton, 'Little Teas for the family' involved slices of bread and butter, dishes of marmalade, jam or honey, 'a standard family cake, one of the "come and cut-me" kind, nice enough for grown-ups, and suitable for the children'. In summer she recommended 'fresh fruit and cream and various ices'.

The China Closet at Tatton Park, with some of the many tea-services on display, along with the 900-piece glass service.

'Buying the Teapot – a bit of Worcester'. By the beginning of the nineteenth century, the purchase of the right teapot was an important part of any lady's shopping expedition. As William Makepeace Thackeray wrote, 'What part of confidante has that poor teapot played ever since the kindly plant was introduced among us. Why myriads of women have cried over it, to be sure! What sickbeds it has smoked by! What fevered lips have received refreshment from it! Nature meant very kindly by women when she made the tea plant: and with a little thought, what a series of pictures and groups the fancy may conjure up and assemble round the teapot and cup!'

Poorer families often had a hotch-potch, mix-and-match selection of whatever they could afford or had been given. In Wales, Marie Trevelyan explained, 'Scarcely a house or cottage in Wales is without a corner cupboard …. In it are kept the household treasures in the shape of teacups and saucers …. It is not at all unusual to see … china cups and saucers of the period when handles were unknown, and teapots that were manufactured when tea was first used.' Nevertheless, the desire to own a complete set was universal. Flora Thompson describes the arrival of a travelling salesman at Candleford:

there was great excitement …. And what bargains he had! The tea-service decorated with fat, full-blown pink roses: twenty-one pieces and not a flaw in any one of them …. Then the glorious unexpected happened. The man had brought the pink rose tea-service forward again and was handing one of the cups round. 'You just look at the light through it …. Ain't it lovely china, thin as an eggshell, practically transparent, and every one of them roses hand painted with a brush?'

The tea service was bought by one of the village men who, only the night before, had returned from his soldiering in India …. Willing hands helped him carry the

tea-service to his home …. His bride-to-be was still away in service and little knew how many were envying her that night.

The British porcelain companies – Minton, Worcester, Derby, Wedgwood, Staffordshire, Chelsea, etc. – were by now manufacturing tea wares in porcelain and bone china. In *Northanger Abbey*, Jane Austen refers to the progress of the porcelain industry:

The elegance of the breakfast set forced itself on Catherine's notice when they were seated at table, and luckily it had been the general's choice. He was enchanted by her approbation of his taste, confessed it to be neat and simple, thought it right to encourage the manufacture of his country; and for his part, to his uncritical palate, the tea was as well-flavoured from the clay of Staffordshire, as that of Dresden or Sève [Sèvres]. But this was quite an old set, purchased two years ago. The manufacture was much improved since that time; he had seen some beautiful specimens when last in town ….

Cups were made with and without handles and saucers were deep. Some social commentators have suggested that at one time it was acceptable to pour the tea from the bowl into the saucer in order to cool it slightly and then to drink from the saucer. This would appear to have been very much a working-class habit that was not approved of by more elegant members of society. The question of the use of the saucer is confusing. It was discussed during the nineteenth century and a comment from that time tells us, 'its first use was believed to be merely to cool the tea, and then it was fashionable to drink from the cup; at a later time the use of the saucer was understood to be confined to saving slops, and thence forward the cup alone was to have the honour of being raised to the lips.' The practice of drinking from the saucer seems to have continued amongst the lower classes, and there are references in contemporary literature to indicate that it continued well into the twentieth century in some homes.

Left: A display of mixed teacups was characteristic of cottages in the nineteenth century. In a glass-fronted bureau in the sitting room at Hill Top in Near Sawrey, Cumbria, Beatrix Potter kept just such a selection of Worcester and Copenhagen cups, alongside Staffordshire and Leedsware jugs and a Staffordshire faun.

Above: An unpublished drawing by Beatrix Potter of Duchess and Ribby for The Tale of The Pie and The Patty-Pan, *1902. Beatrix's Edward VII coronation teapot, with its lid surmounted by a crown, is shown on the table. It can now be seen in the cupboard in the parlour at Hill Top.*

At Killerton House in Devon, the Acland family remembered life in the 1850s:

In those days, tea was very expensive and was kept locked up, in a table. The table contained two wooden caddies, one for green tea, and one for ordinary tea, and one or two large glass bowls, and these all fitted into their places. Grandmama had forgotten her keys and Bronte [the family poodle] was sent to fetch them. In those days, ladies wore white pockets tied around their waists under their dresses. To the horror of the rather prudish people in those days, Bronte reappeared and walked up the dining room, dragging Grandmama's pocket in which were the keys, and Grandpapa used to imitate their horror when he told the story.

Towards the end of the century, when tea was cheaper, lockable ornate caddies for the drawing room were no longer a household necessity. Tin caddies were produced instead for storing tea in the kitchen.

Nineteenth-century tea ware in the drawing room at Mompesson House, Salisbury, Wiltshire. The teapot, sugar bowl and milk jug, all in silver, were made by Hayne & Cater, 1836. The silver tea kettle on its stand was by Robert Harper, 1856. The bone china teacups, saucers and plates were decorated in 1886 by Barbara Townsend, the talented eldest daughter of the family then living at Mompesson House.

As well as porcelain tea-sets, silver or bronze urns, valuable caddies and caddy spoons, upper-class families also owned a selection of silver teapots, sugar bowls, tongs, cream and milk jugs, strainers and teaspoons. For Stourhead in 1812, Sir Richard Hoare had bought from Makepeace & Harker in London a pair of sugar tongs at £1 3s and a silver teapot 'after antique model' for £9 19s 6d. Three years later he purchased a plain silver cream ewer for 5 guineas and a pierced tea strainer with thread fiddle for 2s 8d.

Having decided which tea-set to use, the fashionable hostess then had to choose what kind of table to serve it on. No one particular style developed and designers went on inventing new ideas throughout the nineteenth century. In 1891, *Beauty & Fashion* kept readers abreast of the latest trends with a series of articles. In August, it reported that 'afternoon tea-sets, tables, and trays are a great feature … . They are made in Chinese-patterned china, Hungarian, old blue Dresden or other designs; the tables and trays being tiled to match the tea sets … revolving tea-trays are another speciality.' In November, a second feature told readers, 'Some of the most elegant afternoon tea-tables that could adorn a lady's drawing-room were beautifully made in blue and yellow majolica, designed after the style of Indian wood-carving.' And in December,

the journal featured 'Christmas Novelties at Mssrs Mappin & Webb's': 'A "Surprise Table" was one of the most cute contrivances that we have ever seen. When spread open it held a tray upon which were deposited cups and saucers etc. for afternoon tea. By closing over the wings of the table the tea service vanished beneath, without leaving a trace of its identity; and thus in a moment, tidiness prevails, and in the event of an unexpected visitor appearing upon the scene, there is no necessity for the presence of a domestic to abolish all signs of the meal.'

A teapoy, or casket mounted on a stand for the safekeeping of tea caddies, bowls and spoons. The word 'teapoy' is thought to derive from the Hindu tepai, *meaning three-legged or three footed. This inlaid example, dating from c.1850, was designed by A.W.N.Pugin for Janet Kay-Shuttleworth, and stands in the drawing room of her home, Gawthorpe Hall in Lancashire.*

Lucy and John Jones in the servants' hall at Erddig, home of the Yorke family in North Wales. By the time this photograph was taken in 1943 by Picture Post, *Mr and Mrs Jones were the only staff left – John had begun life at Erddig as a groom, but was now the estate odd-jobman, while Lucy had progressed from nursemaid to housekeeper. The picture is posed, with John wearing coachman's livery, but the tea on the table was part of daily ritual.*

The Twentieth Century

TEA'S UNIVERSAL APPEAL

By the time Queen Victoria died in 1901, tea had become the drink of the masses. Each person was drinking approximately six pounds of tea every year, and by the 1920s, 60 per cent of all world tea exports was being absorbed by Britain. William Ukers, in *All About Tea*, written in the 1930s, observed that

the extent to which tea is drunk in the United Kingdom is surprising, not only to the American or continental visitor but to the Britisher himself who pauses to take stock of his fellow countrymen. Each stratum of British society has its own particular tea-drinking habits and habitats…. Recent social changes in England have caused a spread of early morning and midday cups of tea among domestic servants, shoppers, and business women. Tea drinking at midday is not frequent among the well-to-do, but is common among the working and lower middle classes…. The afternoon tea of the upper classes is the most characteristic of British institutions as well as the most

charming reunion of the whole day; and the afternoon tea of old Betty, the charwoman and laundress, is the most refreshing meal she takes. With the well-to-do, tea-time is the prelude to a late dinner, but with the poor it is the sequel of an early one and so the extremes meet.

Everything, it seemed, revolved around the drink and the meal. The children in J.M. Barrie's play *Peter Pan*, published in book form in 1911, were very clear about their priorities. As Wendy, John and Michael fly to Neverland, Peter Pan offers them the choice of an adventure now, or tea. Wendy quickly decides on 'tea first' and Michael presses her hand in gratitude. Open the pages of almost any light Edwardian novel and you will find tea-parties. A typical story, *A Houseful of Girls* by Mrs George de Horne Vaizey, sets scene after scene around the teapot: 'Maud talked, pouring out tea and dropping sugar into the cups with tragic emphasis', and a few pages later, 'Tea was brought in for the girls' benefit, and Kitty poured it out, spilling the milk over the cloth, and covering the wet spot with the muffin dish with admirable presence of mind. She felt so much at home that she helped herself to cake a second time without being asked, drank three cups of tea and only refrained from a fourth because the pot was drained.'

Even the BBC had to consider carefully when to broadcast certain programmes to fit around tea-time. *The People's Food* said in 1938, 'The hour of the tea-time meal is even more important to wireless broadcasters than breakfast or lunch. The Children's Hour must be fitted in between their return from school and tea-time or postponed until tea is well over. A programme of special appeal to housewives will not secure its maximum listening public if it clashes with the preparation of tea or the washing up.'

Tea in the dining room at Chartwell, Winston Churchill's Kentish home. This photograph taken c.1928 was later used as reference for one of his paintings. From right to left: the painter Walter Sickert, Clementine Churchill, Diana Churchill, Randolph Churchill, Frederick Lindemann (the 'Prof'), Sir Winston, his private secretary Edward Marsh, Diana Mitford and Thérèse Sickert.

TEA IN WARTIME

Tea in the Hospital Ward, *from Stanley Spencer's murals in Sandham Memorial Chapel at Burghclere in Hampshire. Spencer drew upon his memories as a medical orderly during the First World War to paint a series of hospital scenes: this was the last to be produced, in 1932. Bread and jam had been his favourite diet, so the matron always ensured that there was plenty on his ward at the Beaufort War Hospital near Bristol.*

When war broke out in 1914, the government, realising just how important tea was to the British public, was reluctant to impose controls on its supply or purchase. However, by 1917, anxiety about whether there was enough to go around caused people to queue. One woman in Wales who collapsed while queuing was found to have 7lb of tea distributed about her person. The government introduced rationing of foodstuffs such as sugar, margarine and butter, but tea was never rationed.

During the Second World War, tea again played a crucial role in holding the nation together. In 1942, Winston Churchill claimed that tea was more important than ammunition, and the

historian A.A. Thompson wrote, 'They talk about Hitler's secret weapon, but what about England's secret weapon – tea. That's what keeps us going and that's what's going to carry us through – the army, the navy, the Women's Institute – what keeps 'em together is tea.' During the blitz, when people were bombed out of their homes, taking refuge in air raid shelters and on station platforms of the London Underground, mobile tea canteens drove around the streets dishing out cups of tea for anyone and everyone who needed them. Lyons teashops at first closed when sirens blared out their warning of planes approaching, but after a while both public and staff grew impatient of this rule, and carried on until the 'Danger Imminent' signal was given.

Tea rationing was introduced in July 1940 and the rather tight controls hit hard. Lyons teashops immediately arranged to make 100 cups to the pound instead of the pre-war 85. The weekly allowance was 2oz per person over the age of five, which was increased to 3oz for those over the age of 70, with extra allocations for people in vital jobs. Aboard naval vessels, for instance, the sailors always had as many cups of tea as they wanted: Churchill, then First Lord of the Admiralty, had declared that tea was to be issued to them without restriction. By May 1945, the Joint War Organisation, the British Red Cross Society and the Order of St John were sending 20 million or more food parcels to prisoners of war. A quarter pound of tea was always included with cocoa powder, a bar of chocolate, processed cheese, condensed milk, dried eggs, a tin of sardines, and a bar of soap.

Rationed ingredients needed for tea-time had to be carefully and thriftily used. *Home Chat* for July 1940 advertised two little containers to go in a lady's handbag: 'Week-ending away – fulfilling an "afternoon tea" engagement, those precious butter and sugar rations must find a place in your handbag. And for their easy transport we've discovered this clever duet, silver plated, 5s 5d for the sugar container, 9s 9d for the glass-lined butter dish.' Another issue asked readers:

*Do you know how to put those once-wasted dregs into useful commission? Have you ever used strained cold tea for touching up scratches on brown stained floors? Please don't say you never have cold tea left over! You have to admit that there is sometimes a little remaining in your pot, in spite of rationing …. There's your black silk frock, for instance. Sponge it with cold strained black tea and hang it out in the air to dry, and you'll save cleaning bills. Try the same treatment for removing the shine from black or navy skirts … and lastly, those muddy black shoes – they'll be restored to their original smartness in a moment if you wipe them with a cloth wrung out in cold tea …. *

Not a drop, it seems, was to be wasted!

Basildon Park in Berkshire played a noble role in both World Wars. During the latter, British troops used the park for practising tank warfare, Americans completed their training here before 'D' Day. This photograph shows tea-time for the troops with sturdy mugs and doorstep slices of bread amid the Georgian elegance of the Hall.

A wall cabinet from Walter Straw's bedroom at No. 7 Blyth Grove. Medicine bottles fill the lower shelf, and seed and tea measures from the family grocery stores are arranged on the upper shelves

TEA FOR SALE

By 1900, the balance of the origin of the teas being imported to Britain had radically changed. Whereas in 1850, almost all tea came from China, by the turn of the twentieth century, 55 per cent came from India, 30 per cent from Ceylon, approximately 7.5 per cent from Indonesia, and only 7.5 per cent from China. The British preference for a strong coloured liquor led further and further down the black tea route. To satisfy this taste for strong and pungent teas, plantations were established in parts of Africa by the mid-1920s, first in Natal, then Nyasaland (now Malawi), and finally in Kenya – which today supplies approximately 50 per cent of British tea.

By the 1950s, teas being sold to the British public were generally divided into 'Leaf' grades – with subdivisions into Orange Pekoe, Pekoe, Souchong and Pekoe Souchong – and 'Broken' grades – further categorised into Broken Orange Pekoe, Broken Pekoe, Broken Pekoe Souchong, Broken Orange Pekoe Fannings, and Dust – a misleading term which denotes the size of the tea particle.

Tea was landed in the London docks and stored in bonded warehouses on both sides of the Thames close to Tower Bridge. From here, samples were taken and sent out to the various brokers who tasted and valued the teas, then organised for their sale through the weekly London tea auctions. Once the various companies had purchased the tea they wanted, the tea was distributed from the warehouses either direct to retailers around the country who sold the leaf tea loose from the chest, or to blenders and packers who created proprietary blends and sold them packaged in 4oz, 8oz and 1lb packets through grocery stores, door-to-door salesmen, and other retailers.

One small trader who did well from selling tea was William Straw of Worksop in Nottinghamshire. Initially he worked for his brother Benjamin, who had established a grocery business in the town's market place in 1886. Three years later, he bought him out and, in the flourishing economy of the surrounding mining area, the business did so well that William was able to buy the premises he was renting, and to purchase two inns and several cottages. By 1920, Straw was so prosperous that he moved his family from above the shop to a comfortable semi-detached 'villa' at No. 7 Blyth Grove, on the outskirts of Worksop. The house remained in the family until 1990, when William Straw's son, also called William, died, leaving the property with all its contents, and the house next door, to the National Trust.

W. STRAW, Grocer, Tea Dealer & Provision Merchant,
102, MARKET PLACE, WORKSOP.

When William Straw junior left No. 7 Blyth Grove, his home in Worksop, to the National Trust in 1990, the house was filled with reminders of his family's past. This framed calendar for 1893, 'Tit-bits', advertises the Straws' grocery, tea and provisions shop in the Market Place.

Above: Castle Drogo, the 'Norman' castle built by Sir Edwin Lutyens for Julius Drewe with the proceeds from the Home & Colonial Stores. This watercolour painted in 1924 by architectural draughtsman, Cyril Farey, shows the granite building atop a spur of Dartmoor overlooking the River Teign.

Right: Julius Drewe was such a successful retailer that he was able to retire a rich man at the age of thirty-three. He adopted the lifestyle of a country gentleman, as can be seen in this portrait painted by C.M.Hardie. He is shown in his favourite Burberry, preparing to fish on the banks of the Tummel in Perthshire.

The price of tea, at about 2 shillings a pound, was low enough for everyone to be able to afford it. With burgeoning sales and loyal clients, the sale of tea in those early years of the twentieth century brought wealth and fame to many. In the first book of *The Forsyte Saga*, *The Man of Property*, published in 1906, John Galsworthy subtly introduced the fact that tea lay behind at least part of the family fortune: 'Forsyte – the best palate in London! The palate that in a sense had made his fortune – the fortune of the celebrated tea men, Forsyte and Treffrey, whose tea, like no other man's tea, had a romantic aroma, the charm of a quite singular genuineness. About the house of Forsyte and Treffrey in the city had clung an air of enterprise and mystery, of special dealings with special ships, at special ports, with special Orientals.'

In real life, tea dealers did indeed make vast fortunes. With his millions, Thomas Lipton indulged a passion for sailing and socialised with King Edward VII. Julius Drewe's Home & Colonial grocery stores (page 93) had so prospered that in 1910 he was able to retire as a country gentleman and to set about creating a medieval-style castle in homage to his ancestors. Designed by Sir Edwin Lutyens, Castle Drogo sits atop a craggy outcrop in the heart of Devon, a bold and proud testament both to Drewe's

enterprising spirit and to the popularity of tea in the early 1900s.

Clever sales campaigns and advertising became an even more essential part of the business. Brooke Bond used the slogan 'Full weight without paper' to highlight the fact that some companies were cheating their customers by including the weight of packaging in the total net weight of each packet of loose tea. Following the slump of 1929 and the misery and poverty of the early 1930s, the

shop wisely - buy

Brooke Bond
dividend **Tea**

Left: In the 1930s, Brooke Bond introduced the idea of the dividend on a packet of tea, made possible through a direct van distribution system. Customers would save their stamps, valued at a penny each, and hand in their completed cards to their grocer to be given 5s. The vanmen would redeem these sums on their weekly calls.

Below: In the early twentieth century, Brooke Bond mounted a publicity campaign that emphasised they were offering full weight in their packet teas – and implying that most of their competitors had reduced value by including wrappings in the package weight. Empty shops were taken, decorated with promotional material, and free-tastings organised. Notices informed customers that 'if there were no wise folk in Manchester and everybody bought the short-weight packet tea, they would lose 2¼ tons of tea every week, value £336'.

company set out to capture more of the market with the launch in 1935 of their cheap but good quality 'dividend tea'. This was a blend sold in packets bearing dividend stamps that consumers saved and stuck on to a card, ready to exchange for free gifts when the card was full. Typhoo offered a similar scheme that bought savers pens and penknives, doormats, trays, art calendars, tennis rackets and tea trays.

Rosie, one of the chimpanzees who became television stars after their appearance in commercials for Brooke Bond in 1956. Rosie's gastronomic partialities were gin and orange, and almond icing.

The health message also became more important. Brooke Bond's now famous PG Tips took as its name Pre-Gest-Te, emphasising its digestive benefits. Similarly, Typhoo relied on health claims for what they advised was 'digestive and tannin-less – the only true and original Tipps Tea. It is the delicate pure leaf edge'. Leaflets about the negative effects of tannin were slipped inside the packets. Because of its medicinal virtues, Ty.phoo Tipps (the dot was later replaced by a hyphen and the double 'p' became a single in the Second World War) was originally distributed through chemists' shops.

After the end of the Second World War, rationing continued until 1952 and the general quality of teas available was very poor. Once the government's tea controls were lifted, the larger companies gradually took over and the British public was left with four big names – Brooke Bond, Co-op, Typhoo and Lyons Tetley. Smaller companies such as Twinings, Taylors of Harrogate and Matthew Algie still held a place. One established name, Whittard of Chelsea, changed its approach to distribution and retailing and, in the 1980s, became a high street name. But the battle for market share now began in earnest between the major players, using advertising opportunities on public transport, on shop fronts and buildings, and on television with Brooke Bond's famous 'chimps' tea-parties'. Chimpanzees had been associated with the beverage ever since London Zoo organised tea-parties to amuse younger visitors. Now the adverts were given added appeal through the voices of famous comedians and actors, such as Peter Sellers and Bob Monkhouse.

In the 1960s, the introduction of the teabag was to change British tea drinking for ever. The idea is thought to have originated in the United States in 1908 when tea importer Thomas Sullivan sent samples of tea in little silk pouches to clients. His intention was that the leaves should be tipped into teapots in the traditional manner, but the recipients obviously did not understand this and popped the whole bag into the pot, expecting further orders of tea to arrive in the same style. When it didn't, they complained to Sullivan, who recognised the marketing potential and produced the first commercial teabags. By the 1920s, North Americans were brewing most of their tea in bags.

Tea drinkers in Britain were at first disdainful of this practice – the bags were apparently not even brewed in a pot but dangled in a cup of warm water at the table, thus producing an undrinkable brew that barely resembled tea. But, as

'convenience' became the catchword of the 1950s and 1960s, more and more British packers and blenders switched to the bag. In 1968, teabags held an almost imperceptible 3 per cent of the market, but that crept up to 10 per cent by 1970, and 12.5 per cent by 1971. Today almost 90 per cent of tea drunk in Britain is brewed with a teabag.

For the first 15 to 20 years of its life in Britain, the teabag went through various stages of development. Bags were single chamber or gusseted, stapled or heat-sealed, tagged and enveloped, or plain untagged inside cardboard boxes or packets. In the last 20 years, the driving principle to maintain and increase market share led the major companies to rethink the design and shape of the bag. So we saw the launch of the drawstring teabag (to make it easier to squeeze the last drop from the bag before discarding it), the pyramid teabag (to allow the tea leaves as much room to infuse as they would have in a teapot, therefore prompting the question, why not then simply use a teapot?) and the round teabag (to sit more comfortably in the bottom of the cup or mug). One or two of the larger tea companies also started marketing 'instant teas' to combat sales of instant coffee, but the products bore so little resemblance to tea that the take-up was negligible.

Although standard blends in teabags have recently ruled the British market, loose teas are still available. A growing connoisseur market has led to offers of speciality loose-leaf teas from named plantations around the world. And a new interest in organic products has prompted some plantations in the major producing countries to start growing tea without the assistance of pesticides, herbicides and insecticides. By the 1990s, a good range of organic and biodynamic teas was readily available through the main distributors and interest continues to grow.

At the beginning of the twenty-first century, the majority of people in Britain are still drinking black tea. But green tea is also beginning to attract attention, mainly because many consumers regard it as healthier. Smaller speciality tea companies have also added more teas from China to their stock lists to satisfy the demand for the lighter, more subtle flavours of teas such as China Oolong, Pouchong and Keemun. The option of buying by mail order direct from certain retailers or over the Internet has allowed access to a much wider range, turning the clock back to the nineteenth century when teas were imported from China and Japan as well as from India, Indonesia and Ceylon.

Above: Lady on a Sofa, *a pastel by William Hulton. This appears the quintessentially English scene, with tea laid out before the fire, but was in fact sketched in Hulton's home in Venice, the Palazzo Dona.*

Right: Mrs Greville was famous for her tea-parties, and the Tea Room at Polesden Lacey, furnished as a boudoir, was used for intimate gatherings, while the saloon would be used for grander events.

TEA AT HOME

Tea was drunk at regular intervals through the day by the leisured classes of Edwardian Britain. Lesley Lewis, brought up in the early twentieth century at Pilgrim's Hall near Brentwood in Essex, remembered in *The Private Life of a Country House*, 'Our head housemaid called the married couples or single ladies with early morning tea, accompanied by the thinnest of cut bread and butter.' As

the century wore on and the luxury of servants disappeared from many households, the nervous hands of the maid were replaced by an automatic machine called a 'teasmade' that sat beside the bed and, triggered by an in-built timer, boiled the water and bubbled it into the pot that had been set ready with tea leaves. Tea could thus be drunk in private before joining the rest of the household for breakfast, where there would be more tea or coffee.

Afternoon tea for the middle and upper classes was a formal affair, with three-tiered cake stands, and servants delivering and taking away platefuls of sandwiches, thin bread and butter, scones, buttered toast and pastries. Mrs Ronnie Greville was famous for her afternoon teas at both Polesden Lacey, her country house in Surrey, and her London home in Charles Street. In *Down the Kitchen Sink*,

published in 1974, Beverley Nichols described:

the grandest, most formidable, most glittering, and altogether the most impressive tea-table at which I occasionally seated myself.... Tea is at 5 o'clock, and at Polesden, 5 o'clock means 5 o'clock and not 5 minutes past. Which in turn means that the Spanish ambassador, who has gone for a walk down the yew avenue, hastily retraces his steps, and that the Chancellor of the Exchequer, whoever he may be, hurries down the great staircase, followed by several members of the House of Lords, and that the various ladies belonging to these gentlemen rise from their chaises longues on which they have been resting in their bedrooms, removing the perfumed anti-wrinkle pads which they have been balancing on their foreheads, and join the procession to the tea-table which is set out in one of the smaller drawing-rooms.

Home Notes, a women's magazine from the 1930s, told its readers about Queen Mary's tea-parties: 'When the Queen gives an afternoon party at Buckingham Palace, she wears long gloves and no hat, and walks quietly among her guests chatting to them, sometimes accompanied by her daughter-in-law, the Duchess of York, or a lady-in-waiting. Tea is laid in the green drawing room and

the wonderful green-and-white Spode service is used. There is a profusion of flowers everywhere, and the loveliest little cakes, sandwiches, sweets, fruits, and hot scones are laid out invitingly.'

At Wallington in Northumberland, afternoon tea was served in the central hall. Pauline Dower in her memoir, *Living at Wallington*, explained that in her grandparents' time, in time-honoured fashion, 'Lady Trevelyan made the tea herself. Before pouring out each cup she would put a tiny teaspoonful of hot water on the saucer to prevent the cup from slipping about. The milk jug was set on the table – milk was never put in

first! Tea was a delicate meal – very thinly cut bread and butter, small scones (I think already buttered) and cake, all home made, there being no commercial bakers at that time.'

The Great Hall at Packwood House in Warwickshire, showing the table set for the tea in honour of Queen Mary's visit in 1927. Charles Oliver wrote in Dinner at Buckingham Palace, *'the ritual of the English tea-time was brought to perfection by the late Queen Mary, for whom it was the favourite time of day. Everything had to be fully ready by 4pm punctually, with sandwiches, cakes and biscuits invitingly set out on gleaming silver dishes upon a smoothly-running trolley.'*

The delicate arrangement of the food, the fine quality of the porcelains and the elegance of the room were all important elements of perfect drawing-room teas. But so too was the way in which stylish Edwardian ladies dressed for the occasion. While Victorian tea gowns had aimed to give the wearer a little more comfort and ease than her dinner or day dresses offered, with their constricting whalebones and laces, the Edwardian tea gown became a frivolous item of fantasy that allowed ladies to drift from the boudoir to the drawing room with an air of femininity and elegance.

When Edward VII became king, the gloomy atmosphere of dark, stuffy interiors, subdued and sombre colours, heavy furniture, and stiff, formal behaviour was lifted almost overnight. As Sonia Keppel wrote in *Edwardian Daughter*: 'Suddenly all Victorian furniture, ottomans, antimacassars etc. all disappeared. In came chaises longues, papier-mâché chairs, lace curtains, midget tables, nebulous colours .... Whereas in Queen Victoria's reign pater familias predominated and male taste prevailed, now in King Edward's reign, the deification of the feminine was re-established.' And so for tea, the most feminine time of the day, ladies slipped into diaphanous, loose, floating tea gowns (often referred to as teagies!) of pleated chiffon or silk muslin trimmed with lace or satin ribbons, or fringed with crystals, jet, or gold tassels.

In 1902, Mrs Eric Pritchard's *The Cult of Chiffon* offered readers every possible piece of advice as to the design and wearing of tea gowns. 'We cannot', she said, 'trail about the London streets in the flowing garments of beauty, but in our drawing rooms, when the tea urn sings at 5 o'clock, we can don these garments of poetical beauty.' Believing that the tea gown originated in Japan, she advised that the perfection 'may be realised by the combination of Japanese colouring, Grecian lines and French frivolity'. At the beginning of the twentieth century, there was already a widespread interest in oriental design, and the Anglo-Japanese Exhibition held in 1910 in London reinforced the marked influence of the Japanese style on interior and garden design, on fashion and household artefacts, so the idea of a tea gown that resembled a wide-sleeved, loosely wrapped kimono would not have been surprising.

Tea gowns were expensive items, made from luxurious fabrics and trimmings. Mrs Pritchard was very aware of the cost of such garments and offered 'a word of advice to those who have to study economy, always a nasty tiresome consideration in the construction of a tea gown. Silk muslin is wonderfully effective, particularly if you choose it in the special shade that suits you. The "Empire" tea gown is admirable adapted to flowered muslins .... Therefore, there is no need for you girls on a limited dress allowance to sit down and cry because you cannot have my ideal tea gown.'

With the outbreak of the First World War in 1914, the Edwardian 'Golden Age' of elegance and indulgence came gradually to an end and lifestyles changed for ever. Tea gowns slowly disappeared, merging with the 'afternoon frock' or cocktail dress. This was a slightly shorter garment with elbow-length sleeves, a V-neck or apache scarf and long sash that sometimes continued into a short train. Fabrics were still the soft flimsy silks, georgettes, lace and chiffon but the dresses themselves followed simpler and straighter lines.

In the 1930s, ankle-length or calf-length dresses in light fabrics were advertised as 'just right for dancing, supper and tea dates'. Fashion pages used the idea of elegant teas in luxurious surroundings to create poetic and seductive copy to accompany their illustrations. Frocks from Worth were shown as perfect for tea-time on the Riviera: 'Let's away to another part of the world, where the sun shines on mimosa and almond blossoms. In the lounge of a well-known hotel looking out on the blue Mediterranean a group of charmingly dressed girls are waiting for tea.' *Vogue* in July 1930 was delighted that flimsy afternoon frocks were once again appearing at tea-time: 'Last summer, when we dropped into the Ritz for a cup of tea, the ladies to right and to left and behind and before us were nearly all wearing simple rather severe crêpes de Chine. We did a little secret lamenting in our corner about the fall and decline of the gracious tea-hour tradition. A day or so ago, we dropped back into the same room, and it brightened us considerably. The women looked better than they have for years. Delicate materials in soft colours dominated the room.'

By the 1940s, with bombs falling on London and the entire population busy making their own individual war effort, there was no time for elegant afternoon teas. Occasionally fashion magazines included advertisements or articles about 'Hostess, Tea and Individual gowns' for 10 coupons and 13½ guineas, but the tea gown was gradually abandoned.

Below: Fortuny tea gowns. On the left, a blue velvet dress, hand printed in metallic pigment with a design derived from Islamic motifs. The side panels, of finely pleated pongee, are finished with silk cords threaded with Murano glass beads. This gown was purchased c.1911 from Mariano Fortuny's Venice house, the Palazzo Orfei, by Lady Joan Cavendish-Bentinck. On the right, a Delphos gown, dating from the period 1910–20. The Delphos style, first produced by Fortuny in 1907, was intended to be worn with a tunic or gauze cape. This example was made in pleated pongee with pale pink Venetian glass beads.

Above: Cover of Les Modes *magazine, showing a photograph of Madame Rèjane in a tea gown by Doucet, 1902. The gown is of finely pleated chiffon trimmed with lace. The idea of the tea gown was that the wearer might relax and dispense temporarily with corsets and still look extremely elegant. However, it could also be worn as an informal dinner dress over corsets, and here Madame Rèjane's tightly constricted waist is clearly visible through the transparent fabric.*

TEA FOR THE WORKERS

By 1900, tea was the drink of the working classes. There were regional variations, with more coffee being consumed in London and the largest proportion of tea drinkers in Glasgow and Liverpool, but throughout Britain tea reigned supreme. When Beverley Nichols wrote *Down the Kitchen Sink*, he recognised that tea drinking was not the prerogative of the upper classes. After describing Mrs Greville's luxurious tea-parties (pages 156-7), he wrote, 'In spite of the social and historical gap between tea at Polesden and tea in the council house, there is a common denominator linking these two ceremonies – and that is the tea

Above: A civilian canteen during the Second World War, staffed by unpaid members of the Women's Royal Voluntary Service (WRVS). Tea on Service wrote 'the canteens serving that absolutely normal commodity – tea – were oases of calm and a reminder of the every day world. We poured literally gallons of tea into the stricken and the bereaved.'

Right: The staff canteen at Lyons' headquarters at Cadby Hall in the 1950s. The service area was designed with up-to-the-minute stainless steel surfaces, and the seating area offered comfortable but fairly basic facilities for the workers, so that they were not tempted to sit for too long before returning to the factory floor.

itself. The warmth of it, the scent of it, the tang of it. The curious subtle insinuating comfort of it.'

The survey taken by Sir William Crawford and Herbert Broadley in 1938 found that tea was the breakfast beverage for almost 94 per cent of working-class families. At 'elevenses', the mid-morning break, more than 50 per cent drank tea, and at lunchtime tea was again brewed to accompany the midday meal. In the afternoon, the lower and middle classes emulated the upper classes by holding tea-parties as an accepted and economical way in which to entertain friends and neighbours.

Employers in previous centuries had set the precedent and tea continued to be inextricably linked with rest pauses and breaks in the working day. In 1914, a fourteen-year-old girl in service in a chemist's house was allowed 'four slices of bread and dripping with two cups of tea for breakfast, quite a good two course dinner, and a small pot of tea with three slices of bread and margarine for tea'. Servants in large houses took tea in the servants' hall, butler's pantry or housekeeper's room. While Philip Yorke was squire of Erddig in North Wales, the servants' hall was the centre of social activities for all, above and below stairs. Merlin Waterson describes in *The Servants' Hall* how tea was the most important meal, when 'Old actor friends, visiting officials and connoisseurs, distant relatives and part-time helpers on the estate would gather there for mounds of bread and butter, jam and cakes.'

As the century progressed, the working day was slowly shortened, and, since high tea was eaten as soon as the family returned from work, the mealtime came a little earlier. Whereas, before the First World War, it was taken at 6 or 6.30, in the 1930s and 1940s it was more commonly eaten at 5 or 5.30pm. Although high tea was really a lower middle-class and working-class meal, the wealthier classes also served it – especially at weekends for large house parties. Mrs Beeton explained that meals like this 'are governed by the time of the dinner that has preceded them, and the kind of supper to be taken afterwards'. She suggested such foods as 'cake, jam, sardines, potted meats, buttered toast, teacakes and fruit ... bread and butter, and watercress and radishes are nice accompaniments in summer'. By 1950, cookery books were recommending all manner of savoury dishes for high teas. The Good Housekeeping Institute's *High Tea Dishes* suggested 'broad beans with bacon sauce, potato and bacon casserole, vegetable loaf, spaghetti and mushroom pie, cauliflower pie, corned beef fritters, grilled sausages, fish hotpot with cheese and celery, shrimp and hard boiled egg salad'.

The provision of tea in the workplace was now recognised as almost essential to the employees' welfare. In 1916, the Ministry of Munitions' Health Committee stated in a booklet on Hours of Work, 'An opportunity for tea is regarded as beneficial both to health and output'. When the Minister of Labour, Ernest Bevin addressed the Works Management Association in London in September 1940, he told his audience,

I arranged with a great firm to carry out an experiment for me ... I asked them to adopt rigidly the hours I have set down in the circular I had issued; to give ten minutes break in the morning, ten minutes break in the afternoon, with refreshment. The men had to work till seven at night and then there was a very long journey home, so I asked the management to send round barrows of tea at six o'clock in the evening and to see the result.... Now when that experiment I asked for had been going on for a month, I asked the director of the firm if he wanted to give it up and he said, 'Not on your life. I have made too much out of it because of the increased productivity'.

By 1943, over 10,000 factory canteens were making sure that workers got some decent food and plenty of cups of tea to keep them going through their long wartime shifts.

Out of those first official tea breaks sprang the tea trolley, pushed along corridors and up and down office aisles by the ubiquitous 'tea lady', so familiar in factories and offices in the 1950s and 1960s. The Industrial Welfare Society and the Home Office advised in 1925 that 'it will save much time if the drinks are prepared in the canteen and sent round the works by means of trolleys. The advantages of this latter method, both to the comfort of the workers and the good order of the works, are daily becoming more recognised.' By 1942, the same body recommended that 'trolleys equipped with special insulated urns are sent round the departments or tea stations set up at convenient points from which trays can be carried'.

But the 1960s saw the gradual disappearance of the tea lady and the introduction of the first vending

machines in the workplace. The tea that gushed out of these into plastic or paper cups tasted more of cardboard than of tea. The problems of successful brewing inside a convenience machine meant that many opted for coffee or hot chocolate, or sensibly organised the provision of kettles and teabags in the office kitchen. The biggest potential development in the vending machines market came in the 1990s with the launch of hot canned tea sold from counter-top display units in corner shops and convenience stores. But it seemed that British tea drinkers were too discerning to accept the rather odd flavour of tea that had sat around inside a warm metal can for several hours and the idea died a natural death.

Frank Dickens' 1975 cartoon of the tea ladies who were a feature of office life in the 1950s and '60s. Several of his Bristow cartoon strips focused on the important role played by the tea lady and her trolley.

Gesso panel by Margaret Mackintosh (née Macdonald) and decor by Charles Rennie Mackintosh in the Room de Luxe at the Willow Tea Rooms in Glasgow's Sauchiehall Street. Originally called the Salon de Luxe, the middle of the room was furnished with high-backed silver chairs, while lower, curve-backed chairs upholstered in purple velvet stood around the sides. The chandelier at the top left of the photograph was of pink glass, and the wall panels of silver/purple silk decorated with beads.

OUT TO TEA

A Lyons business report written in 1959 looked back half a century: 'the pin-neat Lyons Tea shops were famous all over London. Now the firm was going to earn well and truly Edward VII's attributed remark, "I like Joseph Lyons because he feeds people well ....." The success of the venture soon convinced Lyons that "eating out" for the whole family was not just a popular "craze" but fast becoming an established social habit.'

In Glasgow, Kate Cranston's little empire of teashops was well established when in 1901 she ran a 'tea-house' and 'tea-terrace' at the Second Glasgow International Exhibition. Then, in 1903, she opened the Willow Tea Rooms in Sauchiehall Street (Sauchiehall means 'a damp place where willows grow'). Both the interior and exterior design was the work of Charles Rennie Mackintosh. Created in an old tenement building, the new and exciting approach and wonderful sense of light, with a colour scheme of pink, silver, pale grey and white, gave the shop an impressive feeling of space that thrilled everybody who visited for tea.

Mackintosh's famous ladder-back chairs added a regal touch, and the decorative panels, friezes, lights and mirrors helped to create an overall sense of fantasy. The local newspaper, *The Bailie*, wrote that the shop, 'fairly outshines all others in the matters of arrangement and colour. Indeed Miss Cranston has carried the question of comfort fairly into that of luxury....'

Whereas Kate Cranston set her tables with linen cloths and fine willow-pattern china, ABC shops offered a far more basic interior, with marble slabs and heavier, more durable cups and saucers. James Bone wrote in *The London Perambulator* in 1925, 'I like the ABC shop, although I will admit it has shortcomings. There is something domestic and Victorian about it, an air of plain fare and no nonsense, and food that might do you a power of good.'

Lyons still offered a grander style of catering with plush chairs and palm court orchestras, glamour and opulence. T. Dreiser, an American visitor to London, recorded in 1913 how he remembered venturing into one of the Lyons Corner House restaurants just above Regent Street in Piccadilly, and being struck with the size and importance of it even though it was intensely middle class. 'It was a great chamber, decorated after the fashion of a palace ball-room, with immense chandeliers or prismed glass hanging from the ceiling, and a balcony furnished in cream and gold where the tables were set .... I recall being

amused by the tall, thin, solemn English head-waiters in frock coats, leading the exceedingly bourgeois customers to their tables.'

Lyons were reflecting the style of tea offered in the grand hotels. Many had large airy palm courts, lounges or conservatories where afternoon tea was served every day to the accompaniment of palm court trios, string quartets or gentle piano music. The *Morning Post* for Tuesday 28 January 1908 said of the newly opened Waldorf, 'Once inside, attention is immediately riveted on the spacious Palm Court – a glass covered courtyard treated as a garden, with a marble terrace around decked with light trellis work of a pattern and colour (pale green and white) most restful to the eye.'

In rural areas, owners of cottages with pretty gardens took advantage of the fact that people were increasingly making excursions by bicycle, by train and on foot out of the towns. At weekends and bank holidays, country lanes and seaside resorts were filled with 'day trippers' who needed refreshment during the afternoon and so frequented these local tea gardens. Stylish wooden or wrought iron tables, benches and chairs provided seating on lawns and patios, among rockeries and climbing roses, where lily ponds, classical statues and urns added interest to otherwise modest locations.

Visitors to tea rooms in the early twentieth century could buy postcards to commemorate their visit. The Fullers tea rooms at the London Coliseum (left) is shown in a postcard of 1905. Typical of city tea rooms of the period, the style of the room was elegant, spacious and relaxed, with the waitresses dressed in the traditional black and white.

Tea gardens were a feature of Edwardian England, as increasing numbers took day trips out of cities. The Abbey View Tea Gardens in Tewkesbury, Gloucestershire (right), were furnished with classical statues and urns flanking the path. The Abbey itself can be seen in the background.

Left: Tango exhibition in 1914 at the Argentine and Brazilian Dancing Salon in London. In 1920 the Dancing Times *recalled 'the London season of 1914 ... was the season which witnessed the triumph of the Tango.... Its critics were silenced that night in June ... when Maurice and Florence Walton danced it before the Queen.'*

Below: Dress parade of Paquin gowns at the Palace Theatre, London, on 28 November 1913. The Sunday Times *wrote that the gowns 'represented the last word in the world of fashion'. The headdresses were by Maison Lewis.*

The arrival of the tango from Argentina via fashionable centres in Europe provoked an obsessive interest in the exotic and risqué dance and led to a craze for tango tea dances. The first tango performance in England took place in 1912 on the stage of London's Gaiety Theatre in a show called *The Sunshine Girl*. As a result, everyone wanted to learn to dance it themselves and tango classes were organised all over London in theatres, restaurants and hotels. The *Dancing Times* reflected, 'Tango! Tango! Tango! We are having nothing but tango here now.... We have Tango matinees, Tango teas, Tango suppers.... I wonder will it last.'

The Waldorf Hotel in Aldwych, London quickly became one of the main venues for tea dances. In 1913 Beatrice Crozier described these events in *The Tango and How to Dance It*: 'The Thé Dansants ... in the pretty white and gold ballroom at the Waldorf Hotel, take place on Wednesday afternoon, from half past four to half past seven, and are delightful. Tall white pillars, set out a few feet from the walls down the length of the room, make long colonnades, at either side, which are set forth with small tea tables, where little parties of from two to six can sit and enjoy a most excellent tea between the dances, or remain throughout the afternoon watching the others dance ... .'

The *Daily Express*, reporting yet another event, wrote, 'Tango teas are becoming so great a craze that one wonders if Mrs Brown of Brixton [ie Mrs Average] will ever again be content to stay at home for plain drawing room tea without the accompaniment of a few tangos and a dress parade or two. Yesterday, among London's scores of similar entertainments, came the inauguration of tango teas at the Palace Theatre ...' The dresses in that parade had been specially created by Paquin, the famous French fashion designer. The wide steps of the tango demanded greater freedom for the legs. Skirts were thus shortened and usually split into an elegantly overlapping curve at the front that opened to reveal the ankle and the specially designed tango slippers held in place by criss-cross ribbons that were tied just above the ankle bone.

Beatrice Crozier offered advice about other accessories: 'Bare hands are surprisingly in evidence, for an Englishman can seldom be induced to wear white gloves in the afternoon ... and girls also often seem to take them off for tea and then dance without them ... .' For men, she advised, 'just ordinary

calling dress – black morning coat, dark grey striped trousers, and a black waistcoat, with a white piqué slip in it, and black boots – is de rigueur. Many men wear light spats, and there is no harm in a button-hole.'

The passion for tea dances continued into the early 1920s, but as the smart set grew fonder of the cocktail hour, so tea dances gradually lost their appeal. The Waldorf nevertheless continued with regular public tango tea dances in the

restaurant and these became almost its trademark. When German incendiary bombs fell on the hotel in 1939, the dances came to an end but were reintroduced in 1982 in the Edwardian Palm Court, where they still take place.

The elegant Palm Court of the Waldorf Hotel in 1908 – the year of the grand opening. Still the heart of the hotel, the room is the venue for tea dances every Saturday and Sunday afternoon when a band plays all the favourite dance tunes, including the tango.

Interior of Betty's Tea Rooms in Harrogate. Opened in 1919, this was the first of a chain that now boasts five teashops. The company is still owned by direct descendants of the founder, Frederick Belmont, whose guiding principle was, 'if we want things just right, we have to make them ourselves'.

The 1950s were not a good time for venturing out to tea in Britain. Legislation concerning wages and working conditions made running tea shops much more expensive, and caterers began to turn to self-service coffee bars that apparently met changing public expectations. In January 1955, Allied Bakeries made a successful bid for the Aerated Bread Company shops and restaurants, which then gradually disappeared from London's high streets. The service of afternoon tea in many grand hotels in large towns dwindled to nothing more than a pot of teabag tea and a carelessly-made sandwich or a dull and unappetising piece of pre-packed cake.

However, in some parts of Britain, especially in the West Country, Scotland and Yorkshire, traditions were valiantly kept alive. In Cornwall and Devon, for instance, rich, buttery clotted cream, home-made cakes and pots of 'real' loose-leaf tea brewed in porcelain pots could be enjoyed. In the 1970s, the National Trust began to offer traditional teas to visitors at many of its properties. Having created tea rooms out of kitchens, barns, orangeries, and bakeries, the Trust offered home-baked traditional tea-time treats based on local recipes and often using local ingredients. They recognised that for all British visitors and most foreign ones too, an afternoon wandering around a stately home, castle or wonderful garden is not complete without a cup of tea served with sandwiches, scones and cakes.

In the early 1980s, a gentle renaissance of interest in tea prompted several new ventures – including the opening of my own shop, Tea-Time, in Clapham, London. My two partners and I had no idea that our enthusiasm for tea was part of a trend that was just beginning to manifest itself: for example, a new retail shop called The Tea House opened in London's Covent Garden; the old dairy at College Farm in Finchley, north London, was restored to its original charm to serve wonderful teas on Sunday afternoons. The Waldorf Hotel had reinstated its tea dances a few months earlier, and the Ritz had also started to hold weekend dances. I have often been asked why all these events coincided. Who can say? Maybe it was a reaction against too many fast food cafes and restaurants; maybe it was a sign that none of us really enjoys the fast pace of city life but need those quiet calm moments every now and again.

Despite the new interest, there were very few really good traditional tea places left. In July 1987, *Punch* recognised the problem and commended certain teashops for their quality, 'For a really good tea it is necessary, naturally, to go to

Yorkshire … Betty's tearooms provide an example of excellence rarely equalled. The décor is gracious, turn-of-the-century stuff and the waitresses are dressed accordingly in neat black and white. Their attitude to work also owes something to a bygone age of politeness and decorum.' There were other wonderful places in which to take tea, but you had to know where to go. In London, the elegant lounges of the

Tea-Time in Clapham, south London, which I opened in 1983 with my business partners, David Holmes and Clifford Lee. The 1930s Art Deco theme made it popular with visitors from all over London, and sometimes further afield.

Dorchester and Waldorf hotels were and still are perfect venues for quiet, calming afternoon teas. In Glasgow, the Willow Tea Rooms, set in a re-creation of Rennie Mackintosh's original 1903 interior, and Bradford's, with its black and white-clad waitresses, served excellent tea and tea-time treats. And around Britain, there were a small number of exceptional establishments that kept traditions going and standards high.

Margaret's Tea Rooms at Holt in Norfolk in the 1990s, housed in a seventeenth-century farmhouse. The parlours, the Harebell and the Strawberry, offered traditional teas and home-baked cakes and scones.

It was at this point that American and Japanese visitors became fascinated by the history and traditions of afternoon tea, coming to Britain to try it for themselves. Unfortunately and shamefully for us, they often found themselves sitting at plastic-topped tables in unattractive surroundings, drinking wishy-washy tea that had been brewed with poor quality teabags from thick, heavy unstylish cups – or even worse, from mugs. They must have wondered what all the fuss had been about. The *Daily Express* noticed the trend in April 1985: 'Ever since the poet Rupert Brooke idly enquired over half a century ago "and is there honey still for tea?" four o'clock has been the acknowledged hour when everything stops. Croquet mallets

are laid down, factory machines switched off, and feet all over the country put up in anticipation of a nice cuppa. And as summer approached, tourists flock to our shores looking forward to sampling tea like the English make it. Many of them will be in for a disappointment. Trying to find a decent cup of tea can be as difficult as tracking down a genuine strawberry in the synthetic jam they dish up to plaster our scones.'

The UK Tea Council then stepped in, seeking out quality tea rooms and inviting them to join the Tea Council Guild of Teashops. The Guild's guide-book is published every year with a one-page entry for each outlet. The aim was and still is to help visitors find the best places for tea and not waste their

time in the poorer ones. A network of excellent tea rooms, tea lounges and teashops has been created and is now publicised worldwide. Bruce Richardson, an American writer and tea buff who runs his own tea room in his house in Kentucky, wrote in his 1997 book, *The Great Tearooms of Britain*, 'Tea lovers are quick to recognize shops and restaurants which take their tea service seriously. There is a certain smoothness to the presentation of the freshly-brewed pot. The accompanying scones, sandwiches, and pastries are freshly prepared and displayed with an awareness of visual presentation. The room is inviting and conducive to quiet conversation ... .'

In the mid-1990s, tea was again

threatened by the boom in coffee drinking which led to a rash of fast-service, very modern coffee bars in every high street, railway station, bookshop, clothes store, and shopping mall. Tea fought back bravely and we began to witness the opening of tea bars run on similar lines, offering a good range of the world's finest speciality teas and appealing to both 'eat-in' and 'take-away' customers. The 'Life' pages of the *Sunday Express* included a piece entitled 'Why Tea is the new coffee' in July 1999: 'Almost every street corner now boasts a Seattle Coffee Company, a Costa Coffee, or a Coffee Republic, and it seems all fashionable life is there. But Cool Britannia moves fast and arbiters of style are seeking new caffeine thrills. For them, lattes and americanos are laughably passé. Their taste buds are tickled instead by Darjeelings, Assams and Lapsang Souchongs. Put simply, tea is the new coffee and, in trend-conscious enclaves, stylish new tearooms are springing up nation-wide to cater for the new taste.' When Brooke Bond launched its Ch'a tea bars in 2000, *Tea International* wrote, 'From the silver spoon handle on the front door and the upside-down cup and saucer light shades, to the quirky quotes on all the posters and the limericks on the till counter, Brooke Bond's new Ch'a tea bars are full of energy and fun … . As far as the design of the tea bar is concerned, the approach is that of bringing British tea and tea drinking right up to date.'

Tea Council logo

Page from Woman and Home, *November 1926 issue, showing the fashionable style of tea napkins and table runners that the housewife could embroider. Women's magazines were full of articles about tea wares and tea-time recipes.*

TEA WARES

By the 1900s, most families had tea-sets made up of cups and saucers, sugar bowl, milk jug, teapot, side plates, cake and bread and butter plates, and sometimes a muffin dish. The number and quality of sets depended on social status and wealth.

In *The Private Life of a Country House*, Lesley Lewis described the tea wares used by her grandparents at the family home in Essex during the period from 1912 to 1939:

The fashion in tablecloths changed from plain white to a shade called ecru, both lightly embroidered, then to coarser linen with coloured stripes. In winter, an Art Nouveau covered dish with a blister-pearl finial was put near the fire on a brass tripod and this contained hot scones, buns, crumpets, hot buttered toast or anchovy toast. A wooden cakestand, its three circular tiers folding flat on a rod when put away, held plates and biscuits. On the table would be a plate of thin cut bread and butter, a pot of jam from the Tiptree factory, and perhaps sandwiches. For many years the tea service was white with green and gilt border…. It was followed by a fine Rockingham, a silver-wedding present, in dark pink, white and gold in a chequer pattern, but the breakages in this too-fragile set became tragic and it was replaced by a sturdier yellow-banded Wedgwood. An oval mahogany tray with a shell centre in marquetry, and brass handles was set in front of my mother's place and on this were a reproduction early Georgian silver tea pot, an Irish silver sugar bowl and milk jug on little legs, the china slop bowl belonging to the tea set and the cups and saucers ready for filling and distributing. Hot water was provided by a big silver tea-kettle, a Victorian copy of an eighteenth-century design but so long used and polished that it had acquired the delicacy of an antique.

A 1930s edition of *Mrs Beeton's Cookery* instructed that an '"At Home Tea" is served upon small tables, the servant before bringing it in seeing that one is placed conveniently near the mistress, who generally dispenses the tea. No plates are given for a tea of this kind, and the servant or servants, after seeing that all is in readiness, leave the room, the gentlemen of the party doing all the waiting that is necessary.' Low tables were still preferred for drawing-room teas – just as they had been in Victorian days. Typical of publications of the period, *Woman and Home* included in 1926 an illustration of a 'low Indian brass table – it is just the right height if you are sitting on an easy chair or pouffe'. Tables also came in cane, papier mâché, and Lloyd Loom basketwork, as well as wood.

Mrs Beeton goes on to advise that 'The tea equipage is usually placed upon a silver salver, the hot water is in a small silver or china kettle on a stand, and the cups are small.' On special occasions, when more guests were invited, and musical or other entertainment was also organised, then 'the tea is not served in the drawing-room as at smaller "at homes", but at a buffet in the dining-room, where people go during the afternoon, or sometimes as they leave, to partake of the light refreshments provided'.

Throughout the twentieth century, silversmiths produced a wide range of tea wares – caddy spoons in the shape of jockey caps, hands, and shells, sugar tongs and sugar spoons, boxed sets of tea knives and teaspoons, cake tongs and slices for serving dainty pastries and gâteaux. Covered dishes were designed to keep hot freshly toasted muffins, buttered toast, crumpets and tea cakes. Tea strainers came with or without their own stands. Silver trays were made on which to place a silver teapot and its matching hot water jug, sugar bowl and milk jug.

Teapots have intrigued inventors ever since the beginning of tea drinking and the twentieth century is no exception. All sorts of weird and wonderful creations appeared during the early 1900s. Fenton's patent silver teapot had a basket for the tea leaves which was levered up out of the water once the tea had brewed (1903). The Simple Yet Perfect teapot tipped backwards on to its handle once the tea was brewed in order to separate the leaves from the water (1905). The cube teapot was designed for use on ocean-going liners (1916). The two-spout pot, designed by Lyons, enabled faster pouring in their teashops (1930). And there were pots with ceramic cosies, non-drip spouts, metal spouts, and lockable lids. Manufacturers came up with stackable pots, picnic pots in aluminium (not recommended as a material from which to make teapots), glass pots, electric pots (the first invented in 1909), filter one-cup brewers, and novelty pots in almost every imaginable shape and form – houses, cars, animals, room settings, politicians, pieces of furniture, and pop stars. In the 1900s, pots were elongated and sinuously curved. Minton's 'Secessionist Wares' were influenced by the Viennese Secession Movement, their tall shapes decorated with slip-trailed brightly-coloured patterns. Belleek Porcelain Factory in Northern Ireland manufactured exquisite paper-thin porcelain pots in the shape of shells, coral and sea urchins. Royal Doulton's salt-glazed stoneware seashell teapot of 1907 incorporated shells into the design.

Catalogue from Grimwade Limited of Stoke-on-Trent, c.1920, showing various styles of teapot.

GRIMWADES, LTD., WINTON, ELGIN, STOKE, UPPER HANLEY, and HERON CROSS POTTERIES, STOKE-ON-TRENT.

24's "Simple Life," 1222A.
24's 1/6, 30's 1/4, 36's 1/2.

30's "Simple Life," 2592.
24's 1/7, 30's 1/5, 36's 1/3.

30's "Athens," 1222A.
24's 1/8, 30's 1/6, 36's 1/4.

30's "Wicker," 2656.
24's 1/6, 30's 1/4, 36's 1/2.

30's "Octagon," 6741.
24's 1/8, 30's 1/6, 36's 1/4.

36's "Clarence," 2672.
24's 1/6, 30's 1/4, 36's 1/2.

36's "Hector," 654.
24's 1/9, 30's 1/6, 36's 1/3.

30's "Wicker," 2462.
24's 1/6, 30's 1/4, 36's 1/2.

36's "Simple Life," 1596 U.G.
24's 1/6, 30's 1/4, 36's 1/2.

30's "Clarence," 2697.
24's 1/6, 30's 1/4, 36's 1/2.

30's "Simple Life," 2200.
24's 1/7, 30's 1/5, 36's 1/3.

24's "Salopian," 2656.
24's 1/-, 30's 11d., 36's 10d.

30's "Simple Life," 2461.
24's 1/7, 30's 1/5, 36's 1/3.

30's "Blossom," 2458.
24's 1/8, 30's 1/6, 36's 1/4

30's "Octagon, 2656.
24's 1/6, 30's 1/4, 36's 1/2.

30's "Basket," 2055.
24's 1/6, 30's 1/4, 36's 1/2.

36's "Leaf," 6909.
24's 1/4, 30's 1/2, 36's 1/-.

30's "Tokio," 2462.
24's 1/6, 30's 1/4, 36's 1/2.

Lot No. 3,000.   18 Teapots, 1 each as above, for 21/- the lot.

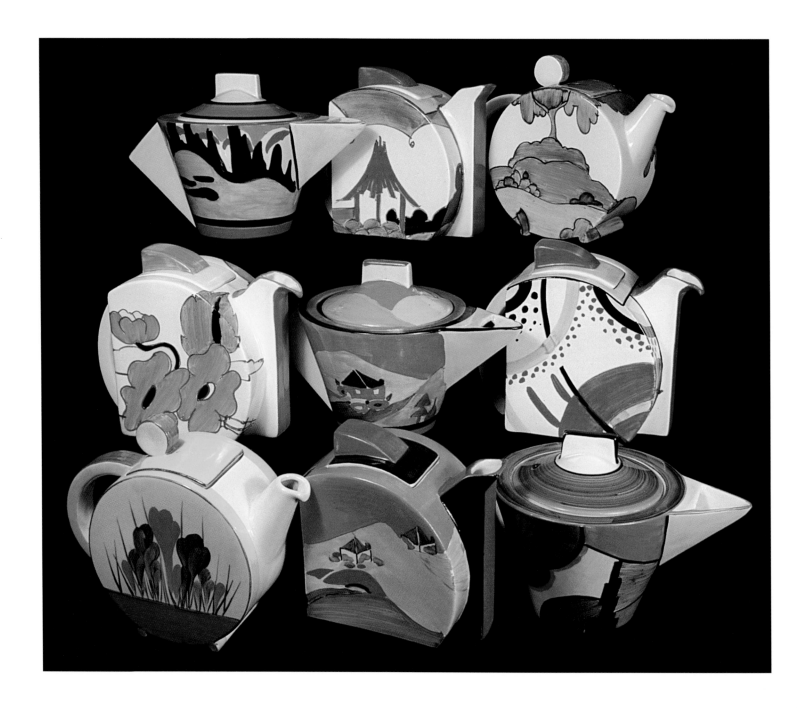

In the late 1920s and 1930s, the teapot was strongly influenced by Art Deco. One woman, Clarice Cliff, was to have more influence than anybody on the designs of the period. Having started her working life as an apprentice in a potbank, in 1916, she took a job at A.J. Wilkinson's works in Newport, Burslem in Staffordshire. Six year later, in recognition of her talent and dedication, she was apprenticed as a modeller and was given the responsibility of decorating the art pottery made at the factory. In 1927, Newport Pottery acquired a warehouse full of poor quality, traditionally shaped wares and Cliff decided that if the flaws were covered over by bright, unusual designs, people would buy them. So she devised her now familiar bold geometric patterns – triangles, naïve representations of fruits, trees and plants, and audacious solid blocks of vibrant colour – that she then used so successfully on her Bizarre range of tablewares. Influenced by the 'Jazz Age' style and by the designs displayed at the 1925 *Exposition des Arts Décoratifs et Industriels* in Paris, she went on to transform the shape of the teapot.

A collection of Clarice Cliff teapots in 'Stamford', 'Bon Jour' and 'Conical' shapes. Top row: 'Appliqué Windmill', 'Summerhouse', 'Rudyard'. Middle row: 'Red Roofs', 'Appliqué Lucerne Orange', 'Carpet'. Bottom row: 'Crocus', 'Appliqué Lugano Orange', 'Sunray'.

While Clarice Cliff was decorating her teapots with vibrant colours and startling patterns, Susie Cooper was adding her softer touch to tablewares. Having started designing in 1924, she set up her own pottery in 1932 and used flowers, fruits, feathers and animals to decorate her stoneware and earthenware teapots. The favourite colours for the hand-painted wares were soft dusty pinks and muted blue-greens against a cream background.

Many British potteries manufactured novelty teapots and sets for children. Wedgwood's Bunny designs, based on Beatrix Potter's stories, were and still are extremely popular. Devonshire Pottery made the famous Simple Simon teapot whose upturned nose formed the spout. Staffordshire's Old Woman Who Lived in a Shoe pot delighted children at tea-time. Shelley produced pots based on the designs of Mabel Lucie Atwell. Beswick Ware had the interesting combination of pots with pictures of Mickey Mouse and Donald Duck riding a tandem, and in the shape of various characters from Charles Dickens' novels. Colclough China Ltd. produced an endearing teapot in the shape of an elephant carrying Sabu, the Indian boy actor, on his back. Sadler made crinoline lady teapots, one of which Queen Mary is said to have owned.

Grimwade's were originally approached by Beatrix Potter to produce clay models of her characters but, becoming more interested in the idea of china teasets, signed a contract in 1918. The company chose the pictures they wanted, and the first results appeared three years later. Beatrix Potter was delighted: 'It is splendid ... far better printed than modern editions of my books.'

Traditional pots were often made with an in-built infuser and in the 1990s, several teapots appeared on the market aimed at connoisseurs who wished to brew their tea with loose leaves and remove them from the infusion before the flavour became bitter. Several companies now offered such infuser pots in iron, porcelain, earthenware, bone china and glass. A range of infusers that fitted almost any vessel was also available. Made from plastic, muslin, metal and paper, many of these were well designed and large enough to allow the leaves to absorb water, unfurl, and release their tea chemicals and flavours into the brew. Smaller novelty infusers in the shape of houses or teapots are often not suitable as they are too small for all the leaves to infuse correctly.

Once the tea was brewed, it was important to keep it hot. Cosies first appeared in the eighteenth century, but acquired a special place at tea-time in the twentieth century as ladies made their own and craftworkers devised new ways of shaping and decorating this practical object. In 1940, *Home Chat* included a knitting pattern with the caption, 'Fresh tea for every latecomer just isn't possible these days, so war-time tea-pots must have their cosies. This quaint cosy in tricot crochet is especially practical as it stays "put" all the time.' A special exhibition, Teapotmania, organised by Norwich Castle Museum in 1995 included a section on craft tea cosies. The accompanying book pointed out, 'The teacosy has always remained primarily a hand-made object ... . The

war, accompanied by clothes rationing, encouraged home sewing and, not surprisingly, patchwork and appliqued teacosies which were made out of oddments of material.' Crinoline ladies and cottage gardens were among the favourite themes. Many of these more elegant tea linens have now been consigned to the attic or sold to antiques markets since they sadly have no place alongside modern methods of brewing and drinking tea.

Tea infusers come in a variety of shapes and sizes: this is a teaball model.

As most tea is now brewed using a teabag, many homes do not possess a teapot. Teabags are simply brewed in the mug from which the tea is to be drunk. However, in recognition of the fact that some people do still prefer to use loose-leaf tea but don't necessarily wish to brew a pot, a range of mugs with their own infusers and lids that work like a mini teapot became available in the 1980s.

Bodum 'Assam' tea infuser. In the 1990s, in recognition of the need to separate the tea leaves from the boiling water once the infusion has reached the perfect strength, Bodum and several other companies started designing a range of teapots with in-built infusers and plungers to make the task of brewing simpler.

TEA TODAY

For the three and a half centuries that the British have been drinking tea, its health benefits have always played an important role. When Thomas Garway first advertised his tea in the 1660s, he made much of the health-giving properties of the beverage. An eighteenth-century paper entitled *The Good and Bad Effects of Tea Considered* claimed that tea 'cools, and allays Drought, helps Digestion, makes clean the Stomach, augments the Velocity of sluggish Circulation, invigorates and gives new Spirits ...'. And by the middle of the nineteenth century, tea had become the symbol of the Temperance Movement. According to Samuel Phillips Day, writing in 1878, 'Philanthropists and sociologists are now fully alive to the moral effects produced by such non-intoxicating drinks as Tea and Coffee.'

Because of those widely recognised benefits, tea has for a very long time also been recommended in folk remedies for such problems as sunburn, puffy eyes, lifeless hair, tired feet and skin problems. In 1940, *Home Chat* told readers, 'Because of the infusion of tannic acid from the leaves, a bottle of strained tea is very useful in the first aid box for dressing burns and scalds. Use two teaspoonfuls to a pint of boiling water,

and apply on pieces of boiled rag, or diluted with an equal quantity of warm water, tea makes a wonderfully soothing gargle for sore throats.'

The health-giving qualities of tea recently took on a new importance. A programme of scientific research co-ordinated by the UK Tea Council proved that tea really does help to protect our bodies from certain diseases. In 1997 it reported, 'Tea cools, calm and refreshes. It provides a very pleasant way of taking in the fluids human bodies need daily for optimum health. It contains trace elements and vitamins, including fluoride, which helps supplement the body's needs, alongside a well balanced diet ... . Importantly, today, there is growing evidence concerning the antioxidants in tea and their role in the prevention of cancer and cardiovascular disease.'

Magazines ran articles with headlines such as 'Cheers to the healthy cuppa', 'Daily cuppa is a healthy option', 'Tea: now the ultimate in fashionable health drinks' and 'How a simple cup of tea can help to beat cancer'. Green tea was perceived to have even stronger powers than black. In recognition, a new range of green tea products started to appear on supermarket shelves in the late 1990s carrying such messages as 'Green teas are naturally low in caffeine and contain

polyphenols which are valued for their antioxidant properties'. Even those who at one time took tea very much for granted now thought of it as a stylish, healthy alternative to coffee and alcohol. They appreciated the fact that it is practically calorie-free, natural and untainted by additives.

Manufacturers of skin-care products and cosmetics also began to consider tea's possibilities for the outer layers of our bodies. Several major international companies launched a wide range of products that included tea extract in their lists of ingredients: sun blocks, anti-ageing creams, moisturisers, night creams, hair shampoos and conditioners and anti-cellulite treatments. Even top perfume manufacturers included black and green tea because of the suitability of the aroma as a base for other essential constituents and because of tea's symbolic importance. Bulgari advertised its *Eau Parfumée* as 'born from the culture of tea and the more profound sense of the rituals tied to it, combining the finest aromas of tea with distinctly Mediterranean fragrances'.

When top fashion designer Donna Karan started selling a range of house-wares in 1997, she promoted her boxed set of Chinese teapot and drinking bowls with the following words, 'Performed with care, the simplest acts can balance and center us. The preparation, serving, and drinking of tea has long been one of the most soothing and satisfying of life's rituals. Slow down. Focus. Find the beauty in life's basics.'

Since the peak of tea drinking in 1959, there has been a slight but steady decline in consumption in Britain. This change may partly be due to the fact that, for many people, tea now has too old-fashioned an image to fit into the fast-paced, sophisticated modern lifestyle of Britain. Tea has found it hard to fight back against the growing popularity of soft drinks such as colas, fruit drinks, and bottled waters, coffee as served in all its different forms in trendy coffee bars all over the United Kingdom, and an increase in the consumption of alcohol. Whereas the *Official History of the Second World War* said that 'People could not run a village dance, raise money for Spitfire Funds, get married or maintain morale in air raids without tea', today alcohol is almost always the preferred beverage for such occasions.

A survey of attitudes to tea carried out for the UK Tea Council in 1993 indicated that older members of society remain more enthusiastic about tea. However, most consumers see it as excellent value for money and the majority of people questioned for the survey regarded tea (in teabags) as an extremely convenient and healthy drink, low in calories, natural and with no unwanted additives, relaxing and reviving, thirst quenching, suitable for all times of the day and all occasions. In an article that appeared in both *The Times* and *Tea International* in 1994, Jonathan Margolis wrote, 'tea continues serenely to dominate our culture, its rituals pervading every area of our social life. The teapot is an icon for all classes ... .'

An icon for all classses – an eighteenth-century teapot from the collection at Saltram.

Select Bibliography

The Book of Tea, preface by Anthony Burgess (Paris)

An Essay on tea, sugar, white bread and butter (Salisbury, 1777)

An Essay on the Nature, Use and Abuse of Tea (London, 1722)

The Etiquette of Modern Society (London, 1881)

Good Housekeeping's 100 Ideas for Breakfast and High Tea (London, 1948)

Tea Gardens and Spas of Old London (from an original text of 1880) (London, 1965)

Tea on Service (London, 1947)

The Good and Bad Effects of Tea Considered (London, 1758)

Acland, Eleanor, *Goodbye for the Present* (London, 1935)

Adburgham, Alison, *Shops and Shopping 1800–1914* (London, 1964)

Archer, Thomas, *Queen Victoria, Her Life and Reign* (London, 1901)

Armstrong, Lucie Heaton, *Etiquette and Entertaining* (London, 1903)

Armstrong, Lucie Heaton, *Good Form. A book of everyday etiquette* (London, 1889)

Austen, Jane, *Mansfield Park* (London, 1814)

Austen, Jane, *Northanger Abbey* (London, 1818)

Austen, Jane, *Sense and Sensibility* (London, 1811)

Austen, Jane, *The Watsons*, manuscript abandoned 1805 (London, 1927)

Baillie, Lady Grisell, *The Household Book 1692–1733*, ed. R. Scott-Moncrieff (Edinburgh, 1911)

Bankes Family Archives, Dorset County Record Office, Dorchester

Barrie, J.M., *The Admirable Crichton* (London, 1902)

Barrie, J.M., *Peter Pan* (London, 1911)

Bartley, Douglas Cole, *Adulteration of Food* (London, 1895)

Bayard, Marie, *Hints on Etiquette* (London, 1884)

Bayne Powell, Rosamund, *Housekeeping in the Eighteenth Century* (London, 1956)

Beeton, Isabella, *The Book of Household Management* (London, 1861)

Beeton, Isabella, *The Book of Household Management* (London, 1879)

Beeton, Isabella, *Mrs Beeton's Cookery* (London, 1939)

Beeton, Samuel Orchart, *Beeton's Complete Etiquette for Ladies* (London, 1876)

Beverley, Michael, *On the Use of Tea and Coffee* (London, 1879)

Bone, James, *The London Perambulator* (London, 1925)

Boswell, Sir Alexander, *Edinburgh, or The Ancient Royalty* (Edinburgh, 1810)

Bott, Alan John, *Our Fathers 1870–1900* (London, 1931)

Boulton, William Biggs, *The Amusements of Old London* (London, 1901)

Bowes, John, of Cheltenham, *Temperance as it is opposed to Strong Drinks, Tobacco and Snuff, Tea and Coffee* (Aberdeen, 1836)

Brewer, John and Porter, Roy, *Consumption and the World of Goods* (London, 1993)

Briggs, Asa, *Friends of the People* (London, 1956)

Brontë, Anne, *Agnes Grey* (1847)

Buchanan, A.P., *A Proposal for Enabling the Poor to Provide for Themselves* (1801)

Burnett, John, *Liquid Pleasures* (London, 1999)

Burnett, John, *Plenty and Want – A Social History of Diet in England from 1815 to the Present Day* (London, 1966)

Burney, Fanny, *Evelina* (1778)

Burney, Fanny, *The Journals and Letters of Fanny Burney*, ed. Joyce Hemlow et al. (Oxford, 10 vols, 1972–)

Butler, Robin, *The Arthur Negus Guide to English Furniture* (1978)

Byng, John, *The Torrington Diaries*, ed. Bruyn Andrews (London, 1954)

Campbell, Lady Colin, *Etiquette of Good Society* (London, 1893)

Campbell, Duncan, *A Poem Upon Tea* (London, 1735)

Carter, Rev. Henry, *The English Temperance Movement 1830–1899* (London, 1933)

Carter, William, *The Power of Truth* (London, 1865)

Chippendale, Thomas, *The Gentleman and Cabinet Maker's Director* (London, 1754)

Clayton, Michael, *The Collector's Dictionary of Silver and Gold of Great Britain and North America* (London, 1971)

Cobbett, William, *Cottage Economy* (London, 1822)

Cooper, Charles, *The English Table* (London, 1929)

Couling, Samuel, *History of the Temperance Movement in Great Britain and Ireland from the Earliest Date to the Present Time* (London, 1862)

Crawford, Sir William and Broadley, Sir Herbert, *The People's Food* (London and Toronto, 1938)

Cross, Arthur Lyon, *Eighteenth Century Documents Relating to the Royal Forest, the Sheriffs and Smuggling* (New York, 1928)

Crozier, Gladys Beatrice, *The Tango and How to Dance It* (London, 1913)

Cuthbert, Alex A., *Memories of Garliestown* (Dumfries, 1908)

Davies, David, *The Case of the Labourers in Husbandry* (London, 1795)

Dawes, Frank Victor, *Not in Front of the Servants* (London, 1973)

Day, Samuel Phillips, *Tea: its Mystery and History* (London, 1878)

Defoe, Daniel, *A Tour thro' the Whole Island of Great Britain* (London, 1724–6)

Dickens, Charles, *David Copperfield* (London, 1850)

Dickens, Charles, *Little Dorrit* (London, 1857)

Dickens, Charles, *The Pickwick Papers* (London, 1837)

Diprose, John, *London Life* (London, 1877)

Donovan, J.P., *Tea in Prose and Poetry* (London, 1929)

Dower, Pauline, *Living at Wallington* (Ashington, 1984)

Drake, Francis Samuel, *Tea Leaves. Being a collection of letters and documents relating to the shipment of tea to the American colonies in 1773* (Detroit, 1970)

Drummond, Jack Cecil, *The Englishman's Food* (London, 1994)

Duncan, Daniel, *Wholesome advice against the abuse of hot liquors* (London, 1706)

Ebery, Mark and Preston, Brian, *Domestic service in late Victorian and Edwardian England* (Reading, 1976)

Ellis, William, *The Country Housewife's Family Companion* (London, 1750)

Emerson, Robin, *British Teapots and Tea Drinking* (London, 1992)

Evans, John C., *Tea in China* (New York and London, 1992)

Fiennes, Celia, *The Journeys of Celia Fiennes 1685–1698*, ed. Christopher Morris etc. (London, 1947)

Fletcher, Ronald, *The Parkers at Saltram 1769–89* (London, 1970)

Forrest, Denys, *A Hundred Years of Ceylon Tea 1867–1967* (London, 1967)

Forrest, Denys, *Tea for the British* (London, 1973)

Forrest, Denys, *The World Tea Trade* (Cambridge, 1985)

Fortune, Robert, *A Journey to the Tea Countries of China* (London, 1852)

Fussell, George Edwin, *The English Countrywoman* (London, 1981)

Galsworthy, John, *The Forsyte Saga* (London, 1922)

Garway, Thomas, *An Exact Description of the Growth, Quality and Vertues of the Leaf TEA* (London, 1660)

Gaskell, Mrs Elizabeth, *Cranford* (London, 1853)

Gaskell, Mrs Elizabeth, *Mary Barton* (London, 1848)

Geijer, Erik Gurstat, *Impressions of England 1809–1810*, trans. by Elizabeth Sprigg and Claude Napier (London, 1932)

Gemelli-Careri, Giovanni Francesco, *Travels through Europe* (1686)

George, Mary Dorothy, *London Life in the Eighteenth Century* (Harmondsworth, 1925)

Girouard, Mark, *The Victorian Country House* (London, revised edition, 1979)

Glanville, Philippa, *Silver in England* (London and New York, 1987)

Godden, Geoffrey Arthur, *Oriental Export Market Porcelain* (London, 1979)

Graham, Frank, *Smuggling in Cornwall* (Newcastle-upon-Tyne, 1964)

Greenberg, Michael, *British Trade and the Opening of China 1800–1842* (Cambridge, 1951)

Griffin, Leonard, *Taking Tea with Clarice Cliff* (London, 1996)

Grosley, Pierre Jean, *A Tour to London* (Dublin, 1772)

Hamilton, Henry, *History of the Homeland* (London, 1947)

Hanway, Jonas, *A Journal of Eight Days' Journey to which is added An Essay on Tea* (London, 1757)

Hole, Christina, *English Home Life 1500–1800* (London, second edition, 1949)

Honey, William Bowyer, *Dresden China. An introduction to the study of Meissen porcelain etc.* (London, 1934)

Houghton, John, *A Collection for the Improvement of Husbandry and Trade* (London, 1693)

Hussey, Christopher, *English Country Houses: Mid-Georgian 1760–1800* (London, 1956)

Huxley, Gervas, *Talking of Tea* (London, 1956)

James, Diana, *The Story of Mazawattee Tea* (Bishop Auckland, 1996)

James, John, *The Memoirs of a House Steward* (London, 1949)

J.B. (Writing-Master) *In Praise of Tea* (Canterbury, 1736)

Kalm, Per, *Account of His Visit to England ... in 1748*, trans. by J. Lucas (London, 1892)

Keith, Edward, *Memories of Wallington* (Paulton and London, 1939)

Kemble, Fanny, *Records of Later Life* (London, 1882)

Keppel, Sonia, *Edwardian Daughter* (London, 1958)

Kerr, Robert, *The Gentleman's House* (London, 1864)

Kinchin, Perilla, *Taking Tea with Mackintosh* (San Francisco and Fulbridge, Maldon, 1998)

Kinchin, Perilla, *Tea and taste, the Glasgow tea rooms 1875–1975* (Oxford, 1991)

Kitchiner, Dr William, *The Cook's Oracle* (London, 1823)

La Rochefoucauld, François, Duc de, *A Frenchman in England 1784*, ed. J. Marchand (Cambridge, 1933)

The Lady at Home and Abroad (London, 1898)

Lettsom, Dr, *The Natural History of the Tea Tree with Observations on the medical qualities of tea, and effects of tea-drinking* (London, 1772)

Levi, Leone, *Wages and earnings of the Working Classes* (London, 1885)

Lewis, Lesley, *The Private Life of a Country House* (Newton Abbot, 1980)

Lillywhite, Bryant, *The London Coffee Houses* (London, 1963)

Lipton, Sir Thomas Johnstone, *Leaves from the Lipton Logs* (London, 1931)

Lyons Company Archives, *The London Metropolitan Archives*

Macdonald, John, *Memoirs of an Eighteenth-Century Footman, 1745–1779* (London, 1927)

MacGregor, D.R., *The Tea Clippers* (London, 1952)

Macquoid, Percy and Edwards, Ralph, *The Dictionary of English Furniture from the Middle Ages to the Late Georgian Period*, 2nd revised edition (Woodbridge, 1986)

Maitland, Agnes, *The Afternoon Tea Book* (London, 1887)

Maitland, Derek, *Five Thousand Years of Tea* (New York, 1982)

Malcolm, James Peller, *Anecdotes of the Manners and Customs of London during the Eighteenth Century* (London, 1808)

Margetson, Stella, *Leisure and Pleasure in the Nineteenth Century* (London, 1969)

Mason, Simon, *The Good and Bad Effects of Tea Considered* (London, 1745)

Mintz, Sydney W., *Sweetness and power, the place of sugar in modern history* (New York, 1985)

Misson, M., *M Misson's Memoirs and Observations in His Travels over England 1688–97*, translated by Ozell (London, 1719)

Montias, John Michael, *Artists and Artisans in Delft* (Princeton and Guildford, 1982)

Morris, S., *History of Temperance Teetotal Societies in Glasgow* (1855)

Morse, H.B., *The Chronicles of the East India Company Trading to China 1635–1834* (Oxford, 5 vols, 1926–9)

Mundy, Robert Godfrey C., *English Delft Pottery* (London, 1928)

Nichols, Beverley, *Down the Kitchen Sink* (1974)

Nye, Gideon, *Tea: and the Tea Trade* (London and New York, 1850)

Nylander, Jane C., *Our Own Snug Fireside: Images of the New England Home 1760–1860* (New Haven and London, 1994)

Ovington, John, *An Essay upon the Nature and Qualities of Tea* (London, 1699)

Palmer, Arnold, *Movable Feasts* (Oxford, 1952)

Pepys, Samuel, *Diary*, ed. Robert Latham and William Matthews (London, 11 vols, 1970–83)

Pimlott, John Alfred Ralph, *The Englishman's Holiday. A Social History* (London, 1947)

Porter, George Richardson, *The Progress of the Nation*, 2nd edition (London, 1847)

Pritchard, Mrs Eric, *The Cult of Chiffon* (London, 1902)

Purchas, Samuel, *Purchas His Pilgrimes* (London, 1625)

Purefoy, Elizabeth, *The Purefoy Letters* (London, 1735)

Reade, Arthur, *Tea and Tea Drinking* (London, 1884)

Richardson, Bruce, *The Great Tearooms of Britain* (Louisville, Kentucky, 1997)

Robinson, E.F., *The Early History of the Coffee House in England* (1896)

Rugg, Thomas, *The Diurnal (1659–61)*, ed. William L. Sachse (London, 1961)

Rugg, Thomas, *Mercurius Politicus* (London, 1659)

Russell, Rex C., *The Water Drinkers in Lindsey 1837–1860* (Barton-upon-Humber, 1987)

Sackville-West, Victoria Mary, *Knole and the Sackvilles* (London, 1922)

Scott Thomson, Gladys, *Life in a Noble Household 1641–1700* (London, 1937)

Scott Thomson, Gladys, *The Russells in Bloomsbury 1669–1771* (London, 1940)

Shore, Henry N., *Smuggling Days and Smuggling Ways* (London, 1892)

Short, Thomas, *Discourses on Tea, Sugar, Milk, Made-Wines, Spirits, Punch, Tobacco* (London, 1750)

Smith, Edward, *Foreign visitors to England and What they have thought of us* (1889)

Sommer, Beulah Munshower and Dexter, Pearl, *Tea with Presidential Families* (Scotland and Connecticut, 1999)

Southey, Robert, *Commonplace Book*, ed. Rev. J. Wood Warter (London, 1849–51)

Southworth, James Granville, *Vauxhall Gardens* (New York, 1941)

Stanley, Liz, *The Diaries of Hannah Cullwick, Victorian Maidservant* (1983)

Strickland, Agnes, *Lives of the Queens of England* (London, 12 vols, 1840–8)

Swift, Jonathan, *Directions to Servants in general* (London, 1745)

Swift, Jonathan, *The Journal of a Modern Lady* (London, 1729)

Swinton, Georgiana Caroline Campbell, *Two Generations*, with a preface, ed. Osbert Sitwell (London, 1940)

Tannahill, Reay, *Food in History* (St Albans, 1975)

Teetgen, Alexander, *A Mistress and Her Servant* (London, 1870)

Tegetmeier, W.B., *A Manual of Domestic Economy* (London, 1875)

Thompson, Flora, *Lark Rise to Candleford* (London, 1945)

Thompson, F.M.L., *English Landed Society in the Nineteenth Century* (London and Toronto, 1963)

Thornton, Peter and Tomlin, Maurice, 'The Furnishing and Decoration of Ham House', *Furniture History Society* xvi (1980)

Trevelyan, George Macaulay, *History of England* (London, 1926)

Trevelyan, Marie, *Glimpses of Welsh Life and Character* (London, 1894)

Tschumi, Gabriel, *Royal Chef* (London, 1954)

Twining, Richard, *Observations on the Tea & Window Act and on the Tea Trade* (London, 1785)

Twining, Richard, *The Twinings in Three Centuries 1710–1910* (London, 1910)

Twining, Stephen H., *The House of Twining 1706–1956* (London, 1956)

Ukers, William, *All About Tea* (New York, 1935)

Ukers, William, *The Romance of Tea* (New York and London, 1936)

Vaisey, David George, *The Diary of Thomas Turner 1754–65* (Oxford 1984)

Von Archenholz, Johann Wilhelm, *A Picture of England* (London, 1789)

Walsh, John Henry, *A Manual of Domestic Economy* (London, 1890)

Waterson, Merlin, *The Servants' Hall* (London, 1980)

Watkin, Pamela, *A Kingston Lacy Childhood; reminiscences of Viola Bankes* (Wimborne, 1986)

Weatherstone, John, *The Pioneers 1825–1900* (London, 1986)

Wesley, John, *Letter to a Friend Concerning Tea* (London, 1748)

Williams, Ken, *The Story of Ty-phoo and the Birmingham Tea Industry* (London, 1990)

The Williamson Letters 1748–1765, Bedfordshire Historical Record Society

Wilson, Constance Anne, *Food and Drink in Britain* (London, 1973)

Wissett, Robert, *A View of the rise, progress, and present state of the Tea Trade in Europe* (London, 1801)

Woodforde, Rev. James, *The Diary of a Country Parson 1758–1802*, ed. John Beresford (London, 1949)

Equivalent values of the pound

This statistical series shows changes in the value of money over the last four centuries, giving the amount of money required at March 1999 to purchase goods bought at £1 at the dates shown on the table.

The retail price index is based on the combined cost of a number of specified goods, and does not, for example, take into account the cost of real property or the level of wages.

UNIT	DATE	TODAY'S EQUIVALENT
£ 1.00	1660	£70.17
£ 1.00	1680	£76.55
£ 1.00	1700	£73.22
£ 1.00	1720	£76.55
£ 1.00	1740	£80.19
£ 1.00	1760	£70.17
£ 1.00	1780	£58.07
£ 1.00	1800	£29.54
£ 1.00	1820	£34.37
£ 1.00	1840	£36.61
£ 1.00	1860	£43.18
£ 1.00	1880	£44.32
£ 1.00	1900	£54.32
£ 1.00	1920	£18.71
£ 1.00	1940	£25.52
£ 1.00	1960	£13.58
£ 1.00	1980	£2.52
£ 1.00	1999	£1.02

List of Plates

The author and publishers would like to acknowledge the many institutions and individuals who have granted permission to reproduce their material in these pages.

Please note that the figures in bold refer to page numbers.

NTPL – National Trust Photographic Library

NT – National Trust Regional Libraries and Archives

65 'Miseries Personal', 1807, by Thomas Rowlandson, from the Caricature Room at Calke Abbey, Derbyshire. *NTPL/John Hammond*

68 'The Country Dance', 1735, by William Hogarth. *British Museum Prints & Drawings*

70 The Castle at Saltram. *NTPL/John Blake*

71 18th-century painting of Cliveden. *NTPL/Courtesy of Viscount Astor*

73 'The Assembly at Bagnigge Wells', 1772, by J. Sanders and J.R. Smith. *British Museum Prints & Drawings*

74 'The Comforts of Bath', 1798, by Thomas Rowlandson. *British Museum Prints & Drawings*

75 Page from Bath Assembly Rooms minute book. *Bath Record Office, Fotek*

77 *The Travellers' Breakfast*, 1824, by Edward Villiers Rippingille. *NTPL*

79 Late 18th-century temperance poster. *Courtesy of Twinings*

80 Oriental tea bowl and teapot, c.1800, at Saltram. *NTPL/Andreas von Einsiedel*

81 Chinese export porcelain, 1720–40, at Stourhead House. *NTPL/John Bethell*

82 (left) Pieces from a Worcester tea service, c.1770, at Saltram. *NTPL/Andreas von Einsiedel*

82 (right) Furstenberg tea caddy, c.1770, at Polesden Lacey. *NTPL/Andreas von Einsiedel*

84 Cartoon, 1825. *Courtesy of Twinings*

86 Detail of the Balcony Room at Dyrham Park. *NTPL/Andreas von Einsiedel*

87 (left) 18th-century tea containers at Clandon Park. *NTPL/Nadia Mackenzie*

87 (right) Late 18th-century tea caddy at Fenton House. *NTPL/John Hammond*

88 An elephant train, photograph taken in 1890s, from *The Pioneers,1825–1900. Courtesy of John Weatherstone*

89 Photograph of a tea auction, 1891. *Courtesy of Wilson Smithett Co.*

91 Poster advertising tea clipper race, 1866. *National Maritime Museum, London*

92 Storage tins at Wimpole Hall. *NTPL/Andreas von Einsiedel*

95 Advertisement for Avoncherra tea. *Author's collection*

96 (above and below) Advertisements for Mazawattee tea. *The Diana James' Mazawattee Collection*

99 The dining room at The Vyne, a 19th-century watercolour by Martha Chute. *NTPL/Derrick E. Witty*

100 (above and below) *'L'Après Dinée des Anglais'*, 1814. *British Museum Prints & Drawings*

103 The Trevelyan family at tea, photograph taken at Wallington in 1899. *NTPL*

104 Late 19th-century photograph of a poor household. *Private collection/Bridgeman Art Library*

105 A Welsh tea party, c.1900. *Museum of Rural Life, Reading*

106 'Kettledrum in Knightsbridge', from the *Graphic*, 1871.

109 The boudoir at Lanhydrock. *NTPL/Andreas von Einsiedel*

110 The servants' hall at Speke. *NTPL/Geoffrey Frosh*

111 'Living off the Fat of the Land', watercolour by Thomas Unwins. *Dreweatt Neate Fine Art Auctioneers/Bridgeman Art Library*

113 The dairy scullery at Lanhydrock. *NTPL/Andreas von Einsiedel*

114 A picnic at Waddesdon Manor, 1880s. *NTPL*

115 (left) Detail of the butler's pantry at Cragside. *NTPL/Andreas von Einsiedel*

115 (right) Queen Victoria in her carriage, from *The Life and Times of Queen Victoria*, 1901, by Robert Wilson.

116 The stillroom at Tatton Park. *NTPL/Andreas von Einsiedel*

119 Detail of the housekeeper's room at Uppark. *NTPL/Nadia Mackenzie*

120 Formal afternoon dress, 1889, in the Killerton Costume Collection. *NTPL/Andreas von Einsiedel*

121 Liberty tea gown, 1897, at Ickworth House, Suffolk. *NTPL/Andreas von Einsiedel*

123 The nursery at Berrington Hall. *NTPL/Nadia Mackenzie*

124–5 Tea party for willow workers, photograph taken c.1900. *Museum of Rural Life, Reading*

125 A tea can. *Museum of Rural Life, Reading*

126 The workhouse at Southwell. *NTPL/Andrew Butler*

127 *Eventide: A Scene in the Westminster Union*, 1878, by Sir Hubert von Herkomer. *National Museums and Galleries, Walker Art Gallery*

128 and 129 (left) Extracts from J.M. Barrie's *The Admirable Crichton*, 1914, with one of Hugh Thomson's illustrations. *British Library*

129 (right) *High Life Below Stairs*, by Charles Hunt. *Christopher Wood Gallery/Bridgeman Art Library*

132 Temperance poster, 1850. *North East Lincolnshire Council, Grimsby Local Studies Collection*

135 Advertisements from *Caterer & Hotel Proprietors' Gazette*, 1894. *British Library, Colindale*

137 C.R. Mackintosh's mural in Miss Cranston's tea rooms, Buchanan Street, Glasgow. *T. & R. Annan, Glasgow*

138 Engraving of a tennis tournament from the *Graphic*, 1892.

139 *Punch* cartoon of Stonehenge, 1897. *Reproduced by permission of Punch Ltd.*

140 Advertisement from the *Caterer & Hotel Proprietors' Gazette*, 1884. *British Library, Colindale*

141 (left) The China Closet at Tatton Park. *NTPL/Andreas von Einsiedel*

141 (right) Mid-19th-century photograph of a family tea. *Victoria & Albert Museum*

142 'Buying the Teapot – a bit of Worcester', an early 19th-century engraving. *Author's collection*

143 (left) Pieces of china in a bureau at Hill Top. *NTPL/Simon Upton*

143 (right) Unpublished drawing by Beatrix Potter of Duchess and Ribby. *Copyright © Frederick Warne & Co, 1955. Reproduced with kind permission of Frederick Warne & Co.*

144 19th-century tea ware belonging to the Townsend family at Mompesson House. *NTPL/Peter Cook*

145 Teapoy designed by A.W.N. Pugin, at Gawthorpe Hall. *NTPL/Mike Williams*

146 Lucy and John Jones at Erddig, 1943. *NT*

147 Tea time in the dining room at Chartwell, *c.*1928. *NTPL*

148 *Tea in the Hospital Ward*, 1932, mural by Stanley Spencer at Burghclere. *NTPL/© Estate of Stanley Spencer 2001. All rights reserved, DACS.*

149 Basildon Park during the Second World War. *NT*

150 Detail from one of the bedrooms at No. 7 Blyth Grove, Worksop. *NTPL/Geoffrey Frosh*

151 Calendar from No. 7 Blyth Grove. *NTPL/Geoffrey Frosh*

152 (left) Watercolour of Castle Drogo, 1924, by Cyril Farey. *NTPL*

152 (right) Portrait of Julius Drewe, 1902, by C.M. Hardie, now at Castle Drogo. *NTPL/Angelo Hornak*

153 (left) Advertisement for dividends. *Courtesy of Brooke Bond*

153 (right) Photograph of shop front advertising full weight tea. *Courtesy of Brooke Bond*

154 Rosie, one of the Brooke Bond chimpanzees. *Courtesy of Brooke Bond*

156 (left) *Lady on a Sofa*, pastel by William Hulton, at Attingham Park, Shropshire. *NTPL/Angelo Hornak*

156 (right) The Tea Room at Polesden Lacey. *NTPL/Andreas von Einsiedel*

157 Queen Mary's tea at Packwood House, 1927. *NT*

159 (left) Fortuny tea gowns from the Killerton Costume Collection. *NT/David Garner*

159 (right) Cover of *Les Modes* magazine, 1902. *Costume Museum, Bath*

160 (left) Civilian canteen during the Second World War.

160 (right) The staff canteen at Lyons' headquarters, 1950s. *London Metropolitan Archives*

162–3 Frank Dickens' cartoon, 1975. *Courtesy Evening Standard and Frank Dickens*

164 Photograph of the interior of the Willow Tearooms in Glasgow. *T. & R. Annan, Glasgow*

165 (left) Postcard of Fullers tearooms at the London Coliseum, 1905. *Author's collection*

165 (right) Postcard of the Abbey View Tea Gardens, Tewkesbury, 1908. *Courtesy of Nigel Temple*

166 (left) Tango exhibition, 1914. *Topham Picture Library*

166 (right) Dress parade at the Palace Theatre, London. *Author's collection*

167 The Palm Court of the Waldorf Hotel, 1908. *Author's collection*

168 Betty's Tea Rooms, Harrogate. *Taylors of Harrogate*

169 (left) Margaret's Tea Rooms, Norfolk. *Author's collection*

169 (right) Tea-Time in Clapham. *Author's collection*

171 The Tea Council logo. *By permission of the Tea Council/FAO*

172 Page from *Woman and Home*, 1926. *British Library, Colindale*

175 Page from Grimwade's catalogue, *c.*1920. *John Johnson Collection, Bodleian Library, Oxford*

176 Collection of Clarice Cliff teapots. *Courtesy of www.claricecliff.com*

177 Grimwade pottery based on Beatrix Potter characters. *Copyright © Frederick Warne & Co. Reproduced with kind permission of Frederick Warne & Co.*

178 Tea infuser. *Quintet Publishing, Ltd., London*

179 Bodum 'Assam' tea infuser. *Countrywide Porter Novelli*

181 18th-century teapot from Saltram. *NTPL/Andreas von Einsiedel*

Index

Numbers in *italic* refer to the captions of illustrations.